Peter Navin and David Creelman
The CMO of People

MW00560230

Peter Navin and David Creelman

The CMO of People

Manage Employees Like Customers with an
Immersive Predictable Experience that
Drives Productivity and Performance

DE
G
PRESS

ISBN 978-1-5474-1663-9
e-ISBN (PDF) 978-1-5474-0051-5
e-ISBN (EPUB) 978-1-5474-0053-9

Library of Congress Control Number: 2018955035

Bibliographic information published by the Deutsche Nationalbibliothek
The Deutsche Nationalbibliothek lists this publication in the Deutsche Nationalbibliografie;
detailed bibliographic data are available on the Internet at http://dnb.dnb.de.

© 2018 Peter Navin and David Creelman
Published by Walter de Gruyter Inc., Boston/Berlin
Printing and binding: CPI books GmbH, Leck
Typesetting: MacPS, LLC, Carmel

www.degruyter.com

To Elise, Charlotte and Max. Three of the most interesting, thoughtful, creative and best people you'll ever meet. Thank you. I love you.

— Peter Navin

I would like to dedicate this to the four people who have played the biggest roles in my career:

My wife, Noraishah, who has been a constant source of support.

Michael A. Thompson whose efforts got me not just my first professional job, but my first four professional jobs.

Don Currie who was my boss at Hay in both Toronto and Kuala Lumpur and taught me all about organizations, consulting and the small French village of Azille.

Debbie McGrath who led me into research and writing as well and showed me what entrepreneurship was all about.

— David Creelman

About De|G PRESS

Five Stars as a Rule

De|G PRESS, the startup born out of one of the world's most venerable publishers, De Gruyter, promises to bring you an unbiased, valuable, and meticulously edited work on important topics in the fields of business, information technology, computing, engineering, and mathematics. By selecting the finest authors to present, without bias, information necessary for their chosen topic *for professionals*, in the depth you would hope for, we wish to satisfy your needs and earn our five-star ranking.

In keeping with these principles, the books you read from De|G PRESS will be practical, efficient and, if we have done our job right, yield many returns on their price.

We invite businesses to order our books in bulk in print or electronic form as a best solution to meeting the learning needs of your organization, or parts of your organization, in a most cost-effective manner.

There is no better way to learn about a subject in depth than from a book that is efficient, clear, well organized, and information rich. A great book can provide life-changing knowledge. We hope that with De|G PRESS books you will find that to be the case.

DOI 10.1515/9781547400515-203

Acknowledgments

Saying "thank you" can be tricky because there are so many people that have contributed, advised, listened and been supportive of this interesting journey.

At the top of the list is Elise Navin. She has listened intently to conversations on this topic for years, read the book at various stages front to back providing great feedback, and has been a major source of encouragement and conviction. Her incredibly simple, clarifying questions forced better thinking and articulation of the concept. Truly an amazing person.

I'm confident the following acknowledgments will not be complete. This is a group of accomplished, interesting people who've made this project very real.

Thank you....

David Creelman for being an amazing collaborator on this project, which was a little over a year in the making. You taught me a great deal about the business of publishing and you have an amazing ability of bringing concepts to life. For sure this CMO of People concept would still be on a napkin or whiteboard if it weren't for our countless hour+ phone interview sessions.

John Boudreau for taking my call, listening to my pitch and ultimately introducing me to David. Our shared HBR project was a great learning process from both a creative and a business model perspective. And your advice to "just publish it" and get moving was spot on.

To our publisher Jeffrey Pepper and Jaya Dalal at De|G PRESS, an imprint of De Gruyter. Your immediate support for the book and great feedback has pushed us to create something we are all proud of. Also, Gary Schwartz through his initial review of our book.

Ann Poletti and Czarina Chung for starting the process of helping me to formally communicate this CMO of People concept to the world at the Glassdoor Conference. Ann is a fantastic storyteller and Czarina's graphic design capabilities consistently exceeded expectations.

To all the leaders that were interviewed for the HBR article and for this book. You dedicated the scarce resource of time and provided valuable insights, incredible anecdotes in support of the concepts, a good market test, and some periodic grounding. This great group included: David Almeda, David Au-Yeung, Paul Baldassari, George Bongiorno, Gregg Gordon, Matthew Guss, David Green, Mike Haffenden, Emma Horgan, Rick Jensen, Phil Johnston, Lucia Quinn, Jacqueline Rese, Dan Schawbel, Amy Skeeters-Behrens, Robert Teed, and Richard Veal.

To two great CMOs, John Boris and Brad Brooks, who've now deservedly gone on to become CEOs. You both were instrumental in giving this concept the necessary space and flexibility to grow and have the impact we all know it could have. In addition to being awesome strategic partners, you often cleared the way in

DOI 10.1515/9781547400515-204

terms of change management process for both the HR and Marketing organizations. And best of all, you made it fun along the way.

Owen Tripp who is creating an industry changing company in a very human way. His "patience first" focus and "assume good intent" mantra are great cornerstones to an amazing culture and brand. Since our first meeting in February 2017, he has been committed to supporting this writing project in part because of his philosophy of a balanced life: work and non-work activities keep a person energized and make for a healthier employee. We've also teamed up to apply the CMO of People concepts in Grand Rounds to enhance the employee experience and build a durable company for the future. His partnership on both fronts is a reflection on him wanting the best for people. He's one of the most genuine leaders you'll meet.

Jeff Housenbold for leading from the front on this concept in its infancy, with investments in the team, shared accountability for its success and business impact, and visible support for the CMO of People model that was new to most folks. He also encouraged me to share the model with other leaders in Silicon Valley and other HR executives. Keith Krach was also an early champion of this approach, which was implemented during an incredible period of global growth at DocuSign.

Dan Springer, Joan Burke and Pete Solvik at DocuSign as well as Christopher North, Jason Sebring and Michael Zeisser at Shutterfly for their collective support from two great companies.

Jose Martin and Susan Otto for reading an earlier version of the book and giving direct feedback that only friends can. As HR executives with a global perspective and a shared desire for the function to improve every day, your input was super important. Rusty Rueff made these lifelong connections happen by assembling a great team at EA. His idea of needing stories to be an effective coach and mentor played a role in the way in which we approached this book: concept to application ("stories") to making progress.

To the amazing employment brand and people analytics team members and pioneers like Stacy Vorkink, Ana Medrano Fernandez, Ann Poletti, Chris Mahar, Mike Euglow, Tony Truong, Arturo Garcia Aguirre, Matt Ketchum and Daschel Benites. Thank you for starting from scratch, testing and fine tuning, building top notch story arcs, brand frameworks and valuable insights into the people that make up the great companies we work for.

Paige Lane and Lauren Shively for masterfully load balancing calendars time and time and again to account for and enable a range of full-time work, advising, writing and family commitments. It's a full life that they help keep on track and on task. In the closing stages of the production process Lauren has played the valuable role of single source of truth to maintain version control.

Contents

Preface

If you are a CEO, how would you rate the impact of your current HR department on business results relative to other key functions? The answer should be that they have a very similar impact. I've had the good fortune of working with a number of CEOs in rapidly growing companies who believed that if HR were run differently it could really drive measurable business results. That conviction allowed me to take on a larger mandate, to elevate the importance and breadth of HR.

Totally reinventing HR was not the game plan when setting out to write this book. As with many of us, my approach is the culmination of experiences over the course of my career. I've chosen to apply many well-worked out concepts from marketing in HR. Both CEOs and venture capitalists immediately see the parallels between the Chief Marketing Officer and the Chief People Officer—that's what led to the term "the CMO of People." They like the concept; intuitively it feels right to them and they know how they could activate it for results.

There is great interest in enhancing the employee experience and bringing other marketing ideas into HR. What I hope makes this book both fresh and useful is that the ideas here have been fully deployed in three organizations. The book is designed to provide the reader with the definition of a concept, its application, and then practical steps to implementation. The two global HR leaders who had a chance to preview the book said the same thing, that it was incredibly practical, that it showed them how to create a predictable, immersive employee experience that leads to productivity and performance. I'd like to think that's true, it was certainly the intent.

I've got to say that this approach isn't for everyone, nor is it the only way people have re-conceptualized the role of HR. I do think the ideas are nicely compatible with what I've heard from thought leaders like John Boudreau and Dave Ulrich. Furthermore, even if you can't bring the whole CMO-of-People approach into your organization, then there will still be parts of the book that will inspire you and that you can make use of.

This book was written for four audiences:
1. Business leaders who know HR should have a bigger impact
2. HR leaders who are looking for a road map to raise HR to the next level
3. Consultants who are intrigued by the analogy to marketing and are looking for some grounding in what has worked in practice
4. Young HR professionals who have the ambition to change the world

DOI 10.1515/9781547400515-206

Comment on Our Use of Pronouns

This book flows from Peter Navin's experience leading HR at Shutterfly, DocuSign, and Grand Rounds. Since the book is based mainly on Peter's ideas and experiences we use "I" as the pronoun throughout. Whenever a concept is mentioned rest assured that it is endorsed by both authors.

Pick up the book and get started.

Peter Navin

Chapter 1
What Is a "CMO of People"?

There is a different way to envision your HR function—and it can be great.

Organizations can improve their performance by changing how they manage people. If you are going to change how you manage people, you are going to want to change how you run HR.

The *CMO of People* concept is a way of framing how we think about the impact HR can have on an organization. We all know what Chief Marketing Officers do: they work to draw in customers, they aim to get the value out of customers, and to do so they seek to create a great customer experience. We should see HR through the same lens: drawing in talent, getting the most value from talent, and doing so on the basis of a great employee experience.

When you map out the duties of a CMO against the duties of a CMO of People (i.e., the head of HR)—as shown in Table 1.1—the analogous nature of the roles is obvious.

Table 1.1: What a CMO Does vs What a CMO of People Does

CMO	CMO of People
Marketing & customer analytics	People analytics
Brand, PR & creative	Employment brand
Customer acquisition	Talent acquisition
Marketing communications	Internal communications
Customer retention	Talent management
Pricing and packaging, marketing strategy	Total rewards
Enablement	Talent operations
Events and PR	Real estate/workplace services

In the companies I've worked for, growth and profitability were critically dependent on having our talent outperform our competitors' talent. The challenge was especially poignant during times of high growth when we had to implement excellent talent management at a breakneck pace. Conceptualizing the HR leader as "CMO of People" helped guide me in my role as head of HR in a fast-growing company and provided a metaphor that the leadership team found fresh, easy to understand, and compelling.

Whereas marketing works the customer funnel, in HR we manage a *talent* funnel, depicted in Figure 1.1, which begins with different channels (including

DOI 10.1515/9781547400515-001

job boards, recruitment agencies, and our career website) that pull candidates into the funnel. Once the candidates are in the funnel, they go through various screening processes to the ultimate transaction: hiring them.

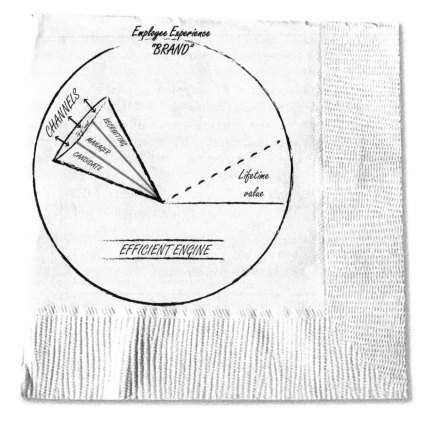

Figure 1.1: The Talent Funnel

Similarly, just as with the concept of a funnel, other marketing concepts like "brand" and "customer's lifetime value" can be translated to HR. In fact, the whole CMO of People concept fits nicely on a napkin and I have used this diagram many times with senior leaders to explain this way of thinking about HR.

Here's how I explain the napkin to a CEO:

- On the left you see the talent funnel as explained in Figure 1.1. The process starts by drawing in a pool of candidates at the top; the hire is complete at the bottom of the funnel and the entire process ends when the person retires or leaves the company. HR's mission is to do a better job than competitors of bringing talent in through the funnel and a better job of enabling employees to add value through their lifetime with the firm.

- After the hire we seek to maximize the "lifetime value" an employee brings to the company over the years they work there. This is analogous to marketing's concept of a "customer's lifetime value" which is all the value a customer brings by buying products and services for all the years they remain a customer. HR's mission is to enable employees to give their best.
- The foundation for a good talent funnel and exceptional employee lifetime value is an "efficient engine" of HR processes supported by the right technology and analytics. The mission of HR is to be sure this engine (that gets the transactional work done) is efficient, so HR can spend time on strategic work.
- Finally, just as all of marketing is surrounded by the ideas of "customer experience" and "brand", so too, all of HR is surrounded by the ideas of "employee experience" and the "employment brand".

This single diagram guides us toward acquiring the best people and enabling them to perform at their best by creating an immersive and predictable employee experience that improves productivity and drives performance. There's a lot packed into that one sentence and it points toward a new way for leading HR.

How to Increase the Employee's Lifetime Value (eLTV)
Exceptional execution in four areas will improve eLTV:
- *Leadership*. People want to be inspired, motivated, and aligned with great executives. Leaders build great teams, and great teams build great companies.
- *Competition*. People want to be on winning teams internally and externally; to build an organization filled with respectful, talented, high performers; and to drive results.
- *Communication*. People want to know what's important to their work; aligning people consistently and continuously with the mission, and priorities, pays massive dividends in the long run.
- *Social Responsibility*. Being proud of yourself, your team, and your company is essential; serving others is the best way to achieve pride.

How do you acquire the best people and enable them to perform better than they have anywhere else? The answer lies in having a solid foundation for the entire model: *the employee experience*. HR needs to develop an immersive and predictable employee experience to improve productivity and drive performance. There's a lot packed into that one sentence and it points toward a new framework for leading HR.

I almost hesitate to use the term HR. It brings to mind a department that only delivers services like training and recruiting, as well as personnel administration and labor law compliance. Yes, an elevated HR function does those things too, but it's not the mission—the mission is to create a competitive advantage through better and more effective talent.

When the mission of HR is framed in this way, the job of the head of HR begins to sound a lot like a CMO. That's why I decided to title this book *The CMO of People*. I've played this role, if not necessarily sporting that title, at three successful organizations. For me, it was the best way to understand the mission, communicate the mission, and establish a framework that enabled us to execute the mission.

The Mission of HR

HR is the group within a company that has expertise in talent. It knows how to find, motivate, and develop talent. It is responsible for a range of different talent processes from recruiting to training to compensation. The mission for HR is to use its expertise and its ownership of talent processes to create competitive advantage that will help the organization achieve its mission.

Being Serious about the Concept of Brand

The nature of the employee experience is captured in the concept of *employment brand*. Many people talk about the employment brand. It's a popular topic. However, too often people think of the brand in terms of a glitzy image. If you are serious about the employment brand, then it will reflect each employees' daily reality. If the brand says that the organization is fun, then employees should be having fun. If the brand says that the organization is dynamic, that should be apparent as soon as you walk in the door.

In the CMO of People concept, the brand is brought to life through an immersive and predictable employee experience that drives productivity and performance. It's a real thing, not an aspiration. It's every*where* (immersive) and every*when* (predictable). It should be as real to employees as Disney's brand is to theme park visitors or as Starbucks' brand is to coffee lovers.

One of the biggest differences between the CMO of People approach and more common approaches to HR is the absolute obsession with bringing the employment brand to life.

What Makes Up the Employment Brand?

Like corporate brands, an employment brand defines the value proposition the company offers to prospective, current, and alumni employees. It's a core part of the overall communication hierarchy of a company that includes vision, mission, and values, and it enables people to better understand what to expect from an employment experience. Values and employment brand work very closely together to paint a realistic picture of what life is like in the four walls each day.

The Link from Employee Experience to Productivity and Performance

All the organizations I've worked in have faced intense competitive pressures. The CEO supported HR's obsession with the employee experience for one reason: that experience brought the best people through the talent funnel and delivered the best lifetime value. The experience naturally had to be a good one for employees, but its success was not measured by employees' happiness—it was measured by the business's growth and profitability.

How do you design an immersive and predictable employment experience that improves productivity and drives performance? You start by looking at each interaction an employee has with an HR process (i.e., each *touchpoint*). What should onboarding do? It should be laser-focused on getting people up to speed quickly and instill the cultural values they'll need to perform. What should workplace services deliver? They should deliver services that remove distractions that harm productivity and should create an environment that the best workers won't want to leave behind. Linking the employee experience to productivity at each touchpoint is not rocket science; it requires focus and discipline.

This intense focus on productivity and performance implies an equally intense focus on data. For example, onboarding isn't assessed simply on whether it *appears* to support the employee experience—the CMO of People wants to see data on how it works in practice.

Not Rocket Science

One of the most important things about the CMO of People approach is that it does not involve rocket science. Yes, the CMO of People cares about analytics, but these can be just the basic analytics that any mid-sized company can afford. Yes, the CMO of People wants the brand to show up in how the company stages a town hall meeting; that doesn't require genius—it just needs someone to ask, "Does how we're running this meeting support the brand?" The know-how to execute the CMO-of-People model already exists in many HR departments.

The approach does demand *design thinking*. Design thinking is a concept from the world of product design. If you want to design a great product you have to think about it as the customer will experience it, and you have to think of that experience as an integrated whole—not as a collection of disconnected features. Design thinking, with respect to HR, rests on two main principles:

- See things through the eyes of the employee's experience.
- Approach issues holistically, with integrated initiatives and cross-functional collaboration.

For example, if you are designing an employee handbook you could potentially just put all the essential information in a binder and make it required reading. However, ask yourself how that may look to an employee: it's a boring activity they are forced to do. A design-thinking perspective would aim to create an employee handbook that employees would want to read that would be aligned with the employee experience the company was trying to grow.

Design thinking forces us to ask how something will impact the employee experience—every time. It also forces us to step back and think about the different elements that affect a project's success, which inevitably means collaborating with departments outside of HR.

What Kind of Person Becomes a CMO of People?

If you are looking to hire a CMO of People or become one, then you should consider the characteristics that stand out in this role. A CMO of People has some particular tendencies:

- *A general management (rather than a functional) perspective.* The CMO of People is part of the core team driving growth and profitability. Yes, they are responsible for an incredibly fun and important part of the business (talent). However, they don't see themselves as the leader of a function; they are a leader in the business—a C-level executive.
- *Risk orientation (implying curiosity and a willingness to learn).* Okay, you've decided to depart from the proven way of framing HR to a new model based heavily on parallels to marketing—that implies an appetite for risk. It also implies fevered curiosity ("I wonder how we can make this work") and a willingness to learn (especially when things go wrong).
- *Collaboration.* It's hard to overstate how tightly linked the work of the CMO of People is to the work of the CMO, CFO, and other C-suite leaders. In this

model, the head of HR is forever sitting in the offices of other C-suite leaders, making sure that everything is aligned and integrated.

- *Systems thinking.* To ensure that the employee experience is exceptional, all the elements of what HR does (and other parts of the business) must fit together. The CMO of People must be a systems thinker—the kind of person who can see how the whole thing can be sketched on the back of a napkin.
- *Data driven.* These days, it almost goes without saying that credible business leaders must have data to back up their decisions.
- *Storytelling.* Data never gives the answer on its own; the CMO of People must look at the mosaic of metrics and craft a compelling story.
- *Adaptability and dealing with ambiguity.* In rapidly growing firms, nothing is clear-cut and nothing stays the same for long. A leader in that kind of environment must be adaptable and comfortable with ambiguity.

The Role of the CEO

It's easy to get excited by the CMO of People approach, but it has to suit the CEO's needs and style. The following conditions must exist for this new HR model to succeed:

- *The CEO must want an elevated HR function.* While they might not say it in so many words, many CEOs don't want to transform HR; they just want an efficient HR function that provides support and keeps HR issues out of their hair. Unless the CEO wants a different kind of HR function, it will be difficult to pursue the CMO of People model.
- *The CEO must be comfortable with the risk.* The CMO of People model leads you toward doing things differently, and that entails risk. At the very least, the CEO will be forced to explain to the board and C-suite why their HR organization isn't doing what other companies' HR departments are doing.
- *The CEO must be patient with change management.* The usual rules of change management apply: It takes twice as much effort and twice as long as you expect to get people on your side. If HR is going to work differently, then a lot of explanation is required. If you embrace the model, the CEO will need to be patient with the effort involved.
- *The CEO must believe the value created can far exceed any costs.* Any change to the status quo will incur costs, but the CEO must have a sense of the value that can be created by elevating HR.

There's an important takeaway here: this approach to running HR isn't for everyone. It's one specific tactic for running an elevated HR function. It's about the CEO, and, as a result, all of the management team, being clear on the need and the impact they are looking for.

Ideas to Watch for

Some ideas regularly pop up in a discussion of the CMO of People approach. As you read the book, keep these themes in mind:

1. *The CMO of People is a part of the leadership team that drives profit and loss.* In this approach, HR and the other functional areas aren't seen as cost centers. The CEO treats the functional heads like a team of general managers.

2. *There is laser-focus on having the highest performing company in which employees can be their most productive.* This parallels marketing's goal of having the most profitable customers (as measured by lifetime value). This goal is achieved through a *differentiated* employee experience that enables productivity and attracts talent. It's not enough to have good talent or to have satisfied talent; the talent must deliver high performance. It's also understood in marketing that you don't get exceptional performance from a generic brand; similarly, the employee experience must be differentiated from competitors. The CMO of People's impact on the business is through increasing productivity and performance, not through "best practice" HR programs and processes.

3. *The employment brand is centrally important to the organization.* The employment brand is not just an outward-facing message to attract new employees; the brand promise is a real fact of life for employees in the organization. The employment brand draws on marketing concepts such as "strategic communication at every touchpoint," "a well-articulated story arc," and "a consistent, predictable experience." A clear brand allows employees to decide if they want to be part of it and creates the conditions for deep commitment.

4. *The primary design consideration for HR activities is the* impact on the end customer *(i.e., the employee).* The HR organization's efficiency is a secondary design consideration.

5. *The CMO of People philosophy accepts taking on risk with surprising enthusiasm.* It embraces the "test, iterate, and measure" approach of product development, rather than a cautious approach that takes pains to avoid mistakes.

6. *The CMO of People, like all other senior executives, insists on having good numbers to support their decisions.* They have the guts to invest in people analytics right away in the belief that, without it, HR won't have an accurate idea of how to have an impact on the business.

7. *The HR organization is elevated in importance, but leaders own the culture.* HR designs the framework for making the company culture come alive; the leaders own it. Leaders cannot use HR as a crutch when it comes to managing people.

What Can You Do Today?

This book has been set up for self-managed learning. The ideas are presented in easily digestible sections. If you are serious about working through this concept, set a schedule for reading each section. Also, take a moment at the end of each section to ponder the "What Can You Do Today?" question. This will guide you to ideas you can implement.

Chapter 2
Impacting the Business as a CMO of People

In this chapter, I'll demonstrate how the CMO of People model differs from traditional approaches. This will help you envision what this model demands of an organization and how it impacts the business.

What Impact Can an Elevated HR Function Deliver?

The point is not to create better HR—the point is to achieve greater business impact.

Thought leaders like professors Dave Ulrich, John Boudreau, and Jeffrey Pfeffer envision an HR function that has a much greater impact on the business than it traditionally has had. In other words, they want to *elevate* the HR function. In many cases the head of HR is part of the C-suite and may have a title like CHRO (Chief Human Resources Officer). The CMO of People model is just one approach for elevating the HR function.

Elevating the HR function gets exciting when we see how it can affect profit and growth. The CMO of People can reach deep into the operations of every part of the organization. This gives the role extraordinary opportunity to have an impact on the organization's success. Let's consider a case of changing strategic priorities: If the organization is shifting to a digital strategy, then the HR team can redesign the organizational structure, identify the managers with the mental agility to handle the new competitive ecosystem, and use incentives to encourage employees to make the transformation work. HR can be an extraordinary platform for a capable executive.

The HR leader has a potentially wider range of impact than any of their C-suite peers. Because of this potential impact, a CEO might make a big bet on who they put in the top HR job—not to mention a big bet in backing them as they shift from the comfortable world of a "support" function to the new world of a "business impact" function. The CMO of People model is one approach for envisioning how such an elevated HR function would operate.

Our example of shifting to a digital strategy is a particularly dramatic case of why a CEO might want an elevated HR function that they could unleash to drive change. However, there are many more routine ways that an elevated people function could impact the business:

DOI 10.1515/9781547400515-002

- Improve operational effectiveness during seasonal peaks by better onboarding of seasonal workers. (Permanent staff will no longer waste time fixing mistakes made by seasonal workers.)
- Reduce the number of bugs in an app by tapping the "talent cloud" of virtual free agents who can do testing. (This will also free up the core IT team to work on the next release.)
- Increase same-store sales by developing more accurate assessments to select better store managers. (In particular, this will reduce the number of new managers who don't last a year.)
- Create world-class products by setting up innovative reward systems that can attract star designers. (This includes people who previously had no interest in working at your organization.)

What other business function has that range of tools in its toolkit? There are no business results that do not depend on people. That's why in the CMO of People model, HR shoulders share accountability for business results. If HR is designed as a support role, the number of bugs in an app is not its concern. However, if HR is elevated, then it certainly will care, and the CIO will rely on the CMO of People and the HR team to do their part by providing the right talent solutions.

Note that I'm not saying that HR has the primary responsibility for matters like same-store sales or bugs; however, neither are they a service function that sits back and waits for a leader to ask them for a tool to access free agents or a new assessment methodology. The mode of working is deeply collaborative. A line manager still owns most of the budget and still has primary responsibility for their staff, while HR's role is to stay right in the mix in optimizing how results are delivered.

Reaching Wide and Deep: The CMO of People's Impact on Profits

A simplified, easy to communicate process that links company strategy to financial targets to strategic priorities has enormous benefits for leaders and teams in organizations large or small. A CMO of People can and should facilitate this roadmap process along with one or two C-suite colleagues. Rusty Rueff, a proven executive in the HR world, demonstrated this best at EA with the annual EA Roadmap. The roadmap fit on one sheet of paper, and from that one sheet anyone could clearly understand the mission, goals, and priorities of EA, one of the greatest entertainment companies. This roadmap can be used at the company level and is easily cascaded into business units, departments, and teams. Today at Grand Rounds, we find this to be a great way to focus and align our emerging growth company as we disrupt the complex healthcare markets. I've also used this approach for each of the teams I've led since my time at EA.

How a CMO of People Handled the 2008 Downturn

We can see how a CMO of People affects the business by looking at a real example. Shutterfly provides customized image publishing for consumers; it's best known for its photobooks. Like every other business, we faced a crisis in 2008 as the economy went into freefall. What would you expect of HR in this situation? At Shutterfly, where I was the CMO of People, the CEO asked CFO Mark Rubash and me to lock arms to focus the company's valuable investments and people on three strategic priorities: photobooks, cards and stationery, and photo sharing.

What tools does a CMO of People have to confront an economic crisis? There are many. In this case, we drew on the power of performance management. We moved performance management to a quarterly (instead of annual) cadence— that aligned everyone on a "crisis" timeframe. Then we realigned incentives and goal setting to zero except for those three priorities that would get us through the crisis.

This process is a good illustration of how design thinking is applied. In this case, the solution involved changing the cadence of the performance management process so that goal setting and performance reviews were done more frequently, and making the process more lightweight by using simpler forms so that it could handle that cadence. We had to change performance management processes, reporting, the supporting technology and communication. Everything had to fit together, and we could only achieve this through tight collaboration between the CEO, COO, CFO and CMO of People, and the rest of the executive team.

We managed to keep growing despite the slowdown. That growth was possible because performance management rigor was instilled across the company, which was a result of the HR function collaborating daily with the CFO and sharing responsibility, along with the entire executive team, of focusing on the company revenue growth. The HR function was a proactive part of the mix, addressing the business crisis as it unfolded, and the CMO of People played a key role in getting the business focused on urgent priorities.

The Opportunity in a Nutshell

The HR organization has the potential to have a dramatic impact on the business. To unleash the potential, the head of HR must play an elevated role with greater accountability and a broader scope than most HR leaders have today.

HR professionals tend to talk about their work in terms of *supporting* the business (such as arranging for executive coaching), running programs (such as an inclusiveness initiative), and managing processes (such as delivering benefits). If you want to elevate the function, then push the HR team to talk in terms of business impact, such as accelerating product development, reducing factory downtime, or increasing per customer revenue. Ask the HR team to post business imperatives, not just HR imperatives, in a prominent place that will keep them top of mind.

Fundamentals of the CMO of People Model

I have suggested that Marketing is a good role model for HR. In this section, I spell out some fundamentals of the CMO of People model.

Three characteristics of the CMO of People model will help to guide the function:
1. Understanding of the brand
2. The range of functions that are included in the HR organization
3. Criteria for success (deciding what not to do)

Let's look at each of these characteristics:

Understanding of the Brand

A CMO of People uses "brand" as a key organizing principle, just like Marketing.

Is brand about image? In part, but it's better understood as a predictable immersive experience that drives greater productivity and performance. Starbucks wants its customers to have a consistent and predictable experience every time they visit a café. To this end, they carefully manage every touchpoint with the customer. Similarly, a CMO of People uses every touchpoint with employees to build a superior brand. They use an "employment brand book" to ensure consistency in interactions with employees, just as Marketing uses a brand book to ensure consistency in interactions with customers.

The point of a marketing brand isn't just to impress customers—the point is to increase sales. Similarly, a CMO of People wants a brand that drives high performance. A traditional HR leader might want the brand to include "a nice workplace"; a CMO of People would want "a workplace that enables performance."

Think about Target's brand—it's not the famous bull's eye logo; it's a comprehensive promise they make to customers. As a customer you go to Target because you know you will find the household goods you want; you know the price will be good; you know you'll be able to find the products easily; and as a result, not only will you go there, but you'll also probably decide to buy something more than you originally planned. It's a predictable experience that is good for the customer and the company. An employment brand should have the same ambitious and comprehensive nature. The employment brand is a critical competitive asset, very much the way the marketing brand is.

In summary, a CMO of People thinks about:
- A consistent and predictable experience
- Careful attention to every touchpoint
- Using the brand to drive performance

These ideas are commonplace in marketing, but business doesn't typically think about the employment brand this way. Adopting these three ideas about brand improves performance. It provides a new way of orienting the attention of the HR department.

Range of Functions that Are Included in the HR Organization

The most visible outcome of this focus on brand is that, in the CMO of People model, HR includes a broader range of functions. In my roles at DocuSign, Shutterfly, and Grand Rounds, three important functions—Real Estate, Communications, and Corporate Social Responsibility—reported to me along with the traditional HR functions.

The rationale is that these functions own significant touchpoints with employees, and therefore have a major impact on brand. The Real Estate function, which is responsible for employees' daily work environment, either has to report to the CMO of People or be highly influenced by the CMO of People. This structure is a natural outcome of the focus on brand as a key competitive tool.

Elevating HR requires some bold changes—increasing the range of functions under HR is one of them. However, this is not a random move; It follows directly from the marketing model, which puts brand at the center.

Criteria for Success (Deciding What Not to Do)

A company can do an endless number of things to potentially enhance the employment brand. How do you choose between them? Consider the following three questions to decide what to do and what not to do:

- *Is it relevant to the employment brand?* Think about this the way a CMO would. It's not enough for an initiative to have some good outcomes; it must reinforce the brand—if it doesn't, pick a different initiative that does.
- *Is it valuable enough to buy?* Think of this from the perspective of the business. Is the HR-offered service or program so valuable that the business would happily buy it from an outside vendor if it weren't being delivered by HR?
- *Is it important to generating ROI?* Think of this from the perspective of the CFO. Will the proposed initiative result in a better ROI than if the time and money were spent on IT or marketing or new equipment? If an HR initiative isn't important to generating ROI then don't propose it.

These seem self-evident, so what makes them special? They're special because people might not like the answers. It's easier to follow "best practices" than it is to hold each proposed initiative up to scrutiny. For example, many people like the idea of awards for long service. If institutional stability is an important part of the brand, then service time might be relevant. In a fast-moving tech company where the emphasis is on rapid change, long-service awards are still nice but not relevant to the business. They get scratched off the list of HR initiatives.

Consider how tempting it is for Silicon Valley firms to "be like Google." With that in mind, they convince themselves that they should follow Google's practice of providing an employee bus. Employees like the perk, but it's expensive—and for most firms, it's not valuable enough to buy. A bus is one of those nice ideas that fails to survive more serious scrutiny.

This does not mean that you shouldn't spend serious money on building scale through HR investments. Shutterfly made the rather bold decision to buy the Oracle HR and Finance modules when the company had only 350 employees. That's a big investment for a small company. What made it relevant and valuable enough to buy was the fact that Shutterfly was in the midst of scaling rapidly. Having that infrastructure made everyone's jobs easier at a time when they needed to focus all their energy on growing the business.

The last question—"Is it important to generating ROI?"—is a reminder to focus on business impact, not HR programs. For example, anything to do with filling positions that, left unfilled, are a bottleneck to growth, is likely to be worth it in terms of generating ROI. Investments in reducing turnover (a perennial favorite issue for traditional HR) only make sense if turnover of good performers is high enough to create undue costs.

What Can You Do Today?

Is the business pushing HR to adopt perks because another company has them? Determine if the proposed perk is relevant to the brand, valuable enough to buy, and important to generating ROI.

Putting a Dollar Figure on the CMO of People's Impact

Do we understand the dollar impact of the HR organization and run our organization based on that understanding?

In the CMO of People model, real estate/workplace services, internal communications, employment brand, and corporate social responsibility functions all report to HR, and HR retains its usual functions. Consider how much financial accountability this implies (see Figure 2.1). The role has direct responsibility for HR spending (items above the line in the diagram) and indirect responsibility and influence over total rewards (items below the line). Overall, the CMO of People role will have an impact on how 40 to 70 percent of the company's money is spent. You should calculate an estimate of these direct and indirect costs in your organization so that you can comfortably quote a number.

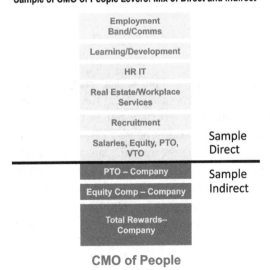

Figure 2.1: CHRO levers

How This Dollar Amount Changes How the Board Sees the Top HR Role

The takeaway is that a business should think hard about HR's role in leveraging this investment. If the HR leader has that much impact, then how much should the board scrutinize them? To what extent should they bear responsibility for the business's growth and profitability? Is it enough to advise the C-suite or do they need to be fully a part of that team?

Many firms treat HR as a cost of doing business rather than as perhaps the most versatile lever for driving performance. Intrinsic to the CMO of People model is the intention to use this lever for all it is worth.

What Leaders from Outside HR Say about Its Impact

The people who seem to best understand the implications of the CHRO levers diagram are CHROs who grew up outside the HR function. Former private equity investor Jacqueline Reses, who became CHRO of Yahoo, and later CHRO of Square, said, "HR was a vehicle for changing the growth trajectory." It's unusual for the board to see HR in that light, but it makes sense when you think of the CHRO levers. Reses also said that HR was a place for "having a view across everybody's business." This tells us both about the size of HR's potential impact and the nature of that impact—if a company is going to use HR to change its growth trajectory, then it must let HR get involved in "everybody's business."

Collaboration as an Action, Not a Value

Emphasizing the large dollar value of HR's potential impact isn't meant to sound like HR should be king of the organization. It's just that the HR organization should be right in the mix with other leaders *collaborating* to solve the problem.

Collaboration can be an empty concept because nobody disagrees with it. If collaboration is just an espoused value, then it may not mean very much. However, we've been discussing how the top HR job could have a huge effect on how the company leverages its expenses. This means that HR must lock arms with the CFO and CMO to ensure a holistic approach to deciding how to spend money. This will show up in the number of hours the CHRO spends with these other leaders; that time will be spent on actively making decisions together, not passively sitting in meetings hearing status reports. Collaboration is not just a nice feeling—it's long hours ensuring that human factors are aligned with all the other elements of a business decision.

One implication of the CMO of People model is that the leadership team will spend its time differently, and work together differently, because that's the only way to leverage the big spend affected by the CHRO. HR can't be off to the side handling its own silo of responsibilities—changing that way of working will make many people uncomfortable.

To evaluate how close your organization is to effectively leveraging HR's direct and indirect impacts, determine how many hours each week the HR head is spending on intense collaboration with other C-suite members. When I was CMO of People, meetings with the CMO, CEO, head of talent acquisition, COO, CRO, and the board dominated my calendar. This meant that I spent less time meeting with the HR team and I gave them an unusual degree of autonomy.

What Can You Do Today?

Put a number on HR's direct and indirect impacts on your organization—a rough estimate is fine. Putting this stake in the ground will help to anchor your view of the magnitude of business impact that your organization should expect from HR.

Next, ask how close your company is to this model of intense collaboration where HR is right in the thick of the decision making, not off to the side. For example, HR weighing in on whether the company could deliver a new product to a customer on time based on HR's understanding of possible staff shortages. How comfortable would the C-suite team be with this approach? Would it slow things down?

Priorities of a New CMO of People

Notice how comfortable a marketer would be with a CMO of People's priorities.

In an organization that is ramping up the HR function under the CMO of People model, four priorities will be top of mind.

1. *Focus HR on where the business is going.* Marketing is naturally inclined toward the future—the next product, the next market, the next repositioning. HR is more naturally inclined toward the present, often in the form of firefighting as HR reacts to urgent requests from business leaders. A CMO of People tries to instill Marketing's future focus into HR. The most important step for creating that future focus is to have HR's goals intertwined with the business plan. HR shouldn't be focused on recruitment or engagement—it should be focused on business goals, such as growth or

time to market. Recruitment and engagement are relevant only to the extent they happen to be, at the moment, the best levers for achieving business goals. Shutterfly's investment in Oracle HR is a good example of future focus—it made sense because HR understood what the company would need to execute its longer-term business plan, even if the heft of the software wasn't needed today.

Determine which HR functions are focused on where the business is going, as opposed to only doing things to keep the organization running in its current form.

2. *Employ analytics, so that investments in talent are based on data.* When HR is tied to driving business success, it is critical that the business context and analytics are at the cornerstone of the project. I'll delve into this in detail in Chapter 5; however, I built the analytics team after hiring recruiters, but before hiring any HR business partners—that's a big reversal of priorities for the HR function. Marketers were forced to shift to an analytics-focused function with the advent of digital media; HR has to follow that lead. A key to making this work is a willingness to bring relevant HR data to the table. If the business needs to make decisions about where to invest, then some data is better than no data. This willingness to start with data, even if it's imperfect, puts HR on the right path.

Measure what you want to become. If having a culture of innovation is crucial to the business, then have that on your dashboard—even if you have to leave the 'answer' to that blank for now. Putting up a blank answer to something important is a better strategy than putting up a detailed answer to something that is of minor interest. If it's an important question and you only have imperfect data, share that data with the business, explain its shortcomings and provide your best advice based on that.

Don't ask whether your HR team is doing advanced analytics—ask whether it is bringing basic numbers to the table as a matter of course. Does HR include analytics in its presentations to the same degree as Marketing, Operations, and Finance, or is it far behind?

3. *Create the total employee experience.* Just like Marketing is fixated on the customer experience, the CMO of People is fixated on the end-to-end employee experience that fulfills the brand promise. It is the guiding framework for attracting talent and driving employees' performance. (I'll cover this in more detail in the next chapter.)

Does your HR function really get this or are there elements of the employee experience that don't come close to living up to the espoused employment brand?

4. Build solid foundational processes. This focus on processes aligns with traditional HR priorities, but with a twist. The twist is that the intent is not just to control costs or ensure that things are running smoothly—although those outcomes matter. The intent is to make sure that HR doesn't get bogged down with things that distract them from their primary goal of ensuring that the business hits its growth targets or other goals.

    Determine whether HR has a roadmap for getting its processes and technologies on track and whether it is executing against that roadmap.

These four priorities should not be too surprising because HR isn't rocket science. You need an HR organization that is clear about how it impacts the business plan and applies rigor to how it does so. HR doesn't always do that because its mandate is to be a support function; Marketing typically does because everyone understands that the point is to drive profitable sales.

What Can You Do Today?

Given how HR tends to get trapped in daily firefighting, pick out one thing that HR needs to do to ensure that it supports the business plan and then confirm that it isn't being derailed by short-term crises.

Stories that Tell the Tale

The following two stories illustrate why you want to elevate HR.

Services-Focused HR: The Millions that Didn't Matter

The HR department of a mid-sized organization was asked about making a change that would result in a $2 million tax-saving over 4 years. They said they couldn't do it. Why? Because they were too busy—or, to be more precise, that was what they believed to be the case, given their understanding of priorities.

It's tempting to blame this HR team for not being business-focused; however, it's fairer to see them as fulfilling their mandate. HR's mandate often does not extend beyond providing services—when a job is vacant, they fill it; when training is requested, they provide it. They were too busy providing services to take on the extra task of saving millions.

If you want an HR department that will jump at a chance to boost the bottom line, then you need to elevate the function. That means creating a mandate that focuses on business impact.

Niceness-Focused HR: Free Cookie Day

I worked in one organization where HR had declared that Wednesday was "Cookie Wednesday." Employees would drop by the lunch room and happily grab a free cookie. It was a benefit. It was nice, but going back to the "criteria for success" in Section 2.2, was it relevant, valuable enough to buy, and delivering ROI? In this case, the issue was not so much cost as relevance. Did free cookies drive the immersive employment brand or was it something that we could stop doing?

Strategically, the company leadership was focusing on a culture transformation from "nice and survivor" to "respectful performance-oriented," so each dollar of employee experience spend was being assessed against delivering that outcome. Cookie Wednesday was not delivering on the outcome—in fact, it was pointed the opposite way; it didn't inspire collaboration, innovation, or community building. We replaced cookie day with activities that embraced friendly cross-functional team competitions in which there were clear winners and losers, curated teams for community building, and a memorable experience for everyone. One popular activity was an "Amazing Race" team challenge. These activities were fun, and more than that, we used the benefit to promote teamwork and a desire to win. We used HR initiatives to drive performance, not to simply be nice.

When HR draws on a marketing framework, it becomes self-evident that free cookie day is not the best use of our time. It's not that a company's success rides on the presence or absence of cookies; when this thinking is multiplied across every employee touchpoint, you end up with a significantly different culture. In this case, we nudged the culture away from one that wanted to eat cookies toward one that wanted to win competitions.

What Can You Do Today?

Are there examples of non-strategic, services-focused HR or niceness-focused HR in your organization? Are you missing opportunities to use HR to drive performance? Is there a framework for HR's role that makes seizing these opportunities a matter of course?

The CMO of People Organization Chart

Here is what the organization chart looks like.

To make things concrete, Figure 2.2 illustrates a CMO of People organization.

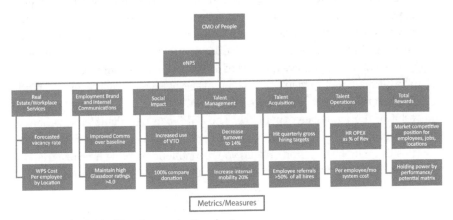

Figure 2.2: The CMO of People organization chart

Notable Features of the Organizational Design

Take a look at the organization chart in Figure 2.2. In many ways it is similar to any typical HR function. However, the following features are worth noting:
- The range of functions reporting to the CMO of People is broader than those typical for a CHRO. Since a strategic imperative is to create and curate an immersive employee experience, the CMO of People must lead these functions. For example, it might be surprising to see an executive director of social impact in the HR organization. However, people who might want to join the company want to know if it is socially responsible; teamwork can be developed using socially responsible offsite events, and paid time off to be a volunteer can be part of the total reward package. When you consider those types of impacts, then you can see why it makes sense to have social impact in HR.
- For the CMO of People to own this range of functions, they must build the trust of their C-suite colleagues. To develop trust, you must have metrics of success. Those metrics are shown on the organization chart. By trust I don't mean whether or not they think you are an honest person—I mean whether

they will trust you to deliver the results the business needs. Without some measures of success, it's hard to trust that anything of value will be delivered.

- Including key metrics on the chart helps direct reports to understand how their work is integrated. In this example, the director of employment brand marketing is responsible for the Glassdoor rating of your organization, yet it is clearly affected by things beyond their control, such as the candidate experience in interviews, the pros and cons of leadership, and the working environment. Even though the senior director doesn't own all those things, they need to be accountable for working with their peers on an integrated plan so that they achieve the goal of meeting the Glassdoor target.

- The ultimate roll-up metric is the Employee Net Promoter Score (eNPS). While we never depend on any single metric, the eNPS is a simple way to capture a lot of the employee experience. The eNPS can be calculated a variety of ways; in essence it's about taking the percentage of employees who respond positively to the question "Would you recommend working here to a friend?" minus the percentage who respond negatively to that same question.

The story of this organization design is a team working together to deliver an immersive, predictable employment experience. The goal of this HR organization can be seen in the design. (Note: I'll leave it to the reader what can be inferred from an organization design where HR reports to the CFO.)

What Can You Do Today?

Look at the organization of your firm's HR department. What "story" does the structure imply? Can you see how each box on the organization chart fits into a coherent, integrated story of how HR delivers business impact?

Examples of How the CMO of People Drives High Performance

I've said that the CMO of People obsesses about business impact. Let's look at a case study of how this works.

A Shift from a U.S.-centric to a Global Business at DocuSign

DocuSign is a technology company that facilitates electronic signatures. In 2014, it recognized the opportunity for extremely fast revenue growth through global expansion. This growth, if fast enough, would result in DocuSign seizing a leading market share in the digital transaction market.

What does going global mean for an HR function? Here's what we did:

- *Employ basic analytics.* Get basic data on the company's global status. How many employees do we have in different locations? How does that compare to what we will need in six months?
- *Engage in talent planning.* The CMO of People, CRO, COO, and CEO began talent planning very early in the process. Forecasts for where we wanted to be in 15 to 18 months were refreshed every six months. Knowing where we were going was crucial; we repressed the desire to just start running. To be honest, it was like hanging on to a rocket through this period—but at least we were hanging on.
- *Recruit talent.* We hired local recruiting talent in each country and used tools (like DocuSign) to accelerate the process of submitting an offer to a candidate and getting them on board.
- *Hit global sales targets.* We partnered with the sales function to understand how long it takes people to ramp up to the point where they can make standard sales quotas.
- *Design a great compensation experience.* We partnered with Mercer to ensure that there were no hiccups in designing and delivering compensation and benefits in all new countries in which DocuSign was operating.
- *Invest in technology that will scale.* We invested in SAP so that the technology could seamlessly scale globally as we became a much larger company. We also knew that there was no way we'd get all the systems integrated right away, so we set up a team of people who were good at aggregating data across systems to plug that gap.
- *Preempt communication breakdowns.* We created an integrated communication program for leaders and employees to ensure that everyone stayed on the same page through this period of hyper-growth. We used various forums to communicate, including email newsletters, town hall meetings, conference calls, information websites, and Chatter groups for the sales team.
- *Preempt loss of culture.* We brought every new employee to Seattle for onboarding to avoid the loss of a coherent corporate culture, which could happen if each location did its own onboarding.

These initiatives called for investments, which were put on the table with all the other proposed business investments so that the leadership team could collectively make an informed decision about priorities.

In the 18-month period from March 2014 to June 2016, the total employee population at DocuSign exploded six times, increasing from 300 to 1,800 people. In the same period, it successfully made the shift from having only 3 percent of its employees outside the U.S. to 35 percent. That change would be difficult to execute without an elevated people function.

Managing Explosive Growth Required Discipline, But Not Genius

The risk in telling this kind of tale is that the audience will either inflate the story so that it looks more sophisticated than it was or underplay the story so that it seems like nothing special. The question to ask is not whether this is sophisticated, but whether it would be executed well given the mandate of most HR functions.

HR is often brought in late during the planning stages, which prevents them from being proactive and gives them a limited understanding of the overall strategic picture. One way DocuSign's key advantage might have been that the CMO of People function was fully integrated into the execution of the business plan and fully committed to its success—not just committed to the success of its HR programs.

It has to be said that going through this hyper-growth is not a pretty process. However, an elevated HR function can get the job done; a positive outcome isn't nearly as likely if the CEO gives the HR organization a limited transactional/operational mandate. If HR is not fully intertwined with the core leadership team, then they'll only get involved in issues (such as talent gaps, cultural breakdowns, or compliance failures) when they become a problem. Waiting until there is a breakdown is no way to run HR since it leaves you with problems that would have been easier to prevent than they are to fix.

What Can You Do Today?

Does this list of HR activities, following from business imperatives, sound like what your HR function is asked to deliver? If not, why not? Is there a gap in how HR is integrated into strategy execution?

The Product Approach to HR Deliverables

Marketing thinks in terms of products—it's a better conceptual model than programs.

How does a marketing mindset change HR? For example, Marketing sees deliverables as products, while HR sees them as programs.

Here are some assumptions that Marketing makes about products:
- The goal is to delight the customer.
- We start with a minimum viable product that will continually improve through rapid iteration.

Compare them to common assumptions about HR programs:
- The goal is to have an administratively efficient process.
- The process will be carefully designed, piloted once, and then rolled out in final form.

Applying Product Thinking to Office Design

Let's consider how I approached the design of the physical workspace. First, as you'll recall from the organization chart in Section 2.6, Real Estate reports to the CMO of People because of its importance to an immersive employee experience. The first question about the physical space was not "How many standard cubicles can we fit into the space?" but "What would it be like to walk into this office?" To put it broadly, the first concern is about how the "customer" (the employee) would perceive the "product" (the office). It's not that we didn't care about costs, nor that another organization wouldn't worry about the employees' perspective, but the CMO of People model that emphasizes predictable, immersive experience helped us to get our priorities right.

The second marketing principle—starting with a minimum viable product and rapidly iterating—showed up in how we approached design. Rather than come up with an office design on paper and then implement, we tested various product features throughout the design process. We experimented with the colors, ambient lighting, and furniture. Once we had a product that delivered the employee experience we needed, we were ready to roll it out to all our locations.

We can apply one of the principles found in the *Fundamentals of the CMO of People Model* section in this chapter here: "Is it valuable enough to buy?" In this context, the question is, "Would a candidate you wish to hire 'buy' this as a place to work?" We made sure the answer was "Yes."

Applying Product Thinking to Town Hall Meetings

You can easily imagine how this product thinking plays out in other initiatives. Consider a town hall meeting (recall that Communication reports to the CMO of People). In your organization, are the speakers and what they want to say the primary perspective? Or is it the employee experience at the town hall? Also, is the design of the town hall meeting always the same or does the company gather feedback each time to continually improve the product?

The product marketing mindset provides a fresh perspective; if you are truly interested in this approach, you'll find that Marketing departments have a whole series of tools to assist with this customer-centric perspective. For example, they create "personas" to capture the essence of different market segments (all customers are not the same). A CMO of People could easily adapt this tool to capture the essence of different employee segments.

Personas

Richard Veal, a line of business leader at Willis Towers Watson, notes that personas are a tool that marketing uses to understand the customer so it's a natural extension for HR to use personas to understand the employee. It usually begins when the company is designing some aspect of the employee experience or is trying to encourage some behavior and thus want some profiles of key representative groups. It's a kind of segmentation, but instead of segmenting in terms of age, gender, or location, you are creating profiles that enable you to segment in terms of hopes, dreams, and desires.

There are various ways to approach creating personas. Veal says that Willis Towers Watson typically starts by analyzing engagement data, then validates the analysis with focus groups of interviews. He cautions that since we are dealing with human beings—and personas are inevitably a simplification—we need to keep an open mind and be alert to feedback.

Examples
There are many ways to communicate a persona. Here is one approach with two personas:

Distinguished Dan

Demographic
- 40–60 year old
- Job Grades 6–9
- 15% of our employee population

Story
- Dan is an experienced and well-established professional
- Confident, loyal, and with a long-term view

Key concerns
- Concerned about how an initiative might interfere with his team's results
- Focused on pension, benefits, and bonus

Messaging tips
- Not interested in details
- Wants to know how it's relevant to him
- Prefers email

Enthusiastic Erin

Demographic
- 25–35 year old
- Job Grades 3–5
- 25% of our employee population

Story
- Erin is an up and coming young professional
- Hungry to learn, eager to get ahead

Key concerns
- Concerned about missing out on opportunity to learn or develop
- Focused on base salary increases and promotions

Messaging tips
- Wants all the details
- Likes instant messaging
- Wants to be able to ask questions

The descriptions of Enthusiatic Erin and Distinguished Dan are fictitious; the photos are in the public domain.

What Can You Do Today?

The product metaphor is simple, but if the HR culture thinks of deliverables solely in terms of programs, it can be difficult to see the world through a marketer's eyes. The easiest thing to do is to get someone experienced in product marketing involved in the next HR initiative. This could be formal involvement on a cross-functional team, or informally seeking counsel over a cup of coffee from someone with the appropriate product mindset.

Challenges of Bringing the CMO of People Model to an Organization

CEOs should know some things before adopting the CMO of People model.
CEOs must confront the key fact that a CMO of People will put significant demands on them. Instead of shielding the CEO from HR issues, a CMO of People will bring people's issues to the center of strategic discussions. The model adds a high-powered leader to the inner circle. It means doing things differently from other companies, which will force the CEO to back the CMO of People when they take on unusual and risky projects. The model is a powerful way to create business impact, though not an easy one to execute.

Why DocuSign and Shutterfly Embarked on This Journey

Both DocuSign and Shutterfly were rapidly growing technology companies. This meant that the needs for top talent and ongoing transformation were evident to the top team. The CEOs asked me to lead this task of transforming talent management and to bring a strategic perspective to this project.

Coming from a non-HR background, ideas like "end-to-end employee experience" and "sustainable brand" were natural ways to frame HR's objectives. The "CMO of People" title was an obvious way to signal that I was taking a different approach.

My CEOs liked the CMO of People model because they understood the CMO's role and why it had strategic value. They hadn't necessarily seen an HR function elevated to this strategic level so the CHRO term was not as evocative to them. The CMO of People concept wasn't just useful as a framework for running HR—it was useful for getting the whole organization to see HR in a new light.

How Other Managers Reacted

Many of our senior leaders hadn't seen HR run this way, so it was a learning experience for them too. It takes time for people to see how things fit together and why it makes sense to do it this way. In Chapter 5, I'll talk about prioritizing analytics, a choice that meant we would go without HR business partners for some time. Managers would say, "Where's my HR business partner? I've always had one in every other place I've worked. Why don't we have that here?" It's not that I disagreed that they needed an HR business partner, just that we could only do so much and analytics was a higher priority. HR business partners were hired later on as the business grew.

Getting managers on your side is a matter of change management, which means doing a lot of explaining on an ongoing basis.

The Need to Elevate Collaboration

There are two types of leaders who will struggle under the CMO of People model. One is the leader who is used to HR being half a step down from the other C-suite roles and hence more focused on providing support than collaborating on decisions. The other is the leader who is used to making the HR decisions without having to hash them out with another C-suite leader.

A curious feature of the CMO of People model is that while the role has a lot of leverage, it is also highly dependent on the other members of the C-suite team. For example, I've talked a lot about the importance of the employment brand; however, the head of HR doesn't create that on their own. In my work, I needed a truly great relationship with the CMO; we needed a shared vision of the brand that encompassed both product and employees. The CMO and the CMO of People both signed off on the company's employment "brand book."

Collaboration was also essential in real estate/workplace services. This function reported to the CMO of People because it was central to the end-to-end employee experience. However, the CFO needed to be part of the discussion because it involved a lot of money. Similarly, the CRO and COO needed to be involved because they owned 80 percent of the workforce. HR sits within a decision-making team.

Collaboration shouldn't be confused with abdication, where HR just goes along with what other functions want. HR must own its responsibilities without underestimating the importance of having others involved in the decision making. The collaboration should be almost invisible—when it feels this way, you know that it's working.

What I Did Wrong

It's useful to look back and see what I could have done differently. Here is what I think I could have done better:

- In retrospect, it took me too long to articulate the CMO of People philosophy. When I reached the point of having clearly artic-ulated this strategy, it became much easier to know what I should and shouldn't be doing, and then explain that to people. At Shutterfly I initially felt my ideas were clear, but it became obvious that others didn't find them as clear as I thought they were! As I kept practicing my explanation of the approach of my philosophy, it became clearer to me as well. This continual work on practicing how to explain ideas is a necessary process; once it's done and you can articulate the ideas easily, it makes it easier for others to get on board.

- I wish I had known how much change management would be involved. If you had asked me at the time, I would have told you "a lot," but that still greatly underestimated what was involved. There is an old rule that you have to repeat something seven times before it will stick. Perhaps a more concrete example of that is that when you explain a new concept, people get it after a few repetitions. However, as soon as you get to the practical application in the workplace and you try to do something different so that it aligns with the new philosophy, people will stop you and ask why you are making a change from what they expected. You have to go back and reiterate the philosophy and then demonstrate how it leads to the change. For example, we might have a role called "employee brand director" and they would be given responsibility for the company's Glassdoor ratings. The marketing department might ask why this person was worried about Glassdoor ratings since, previously, only marketing was watching that data. As the CMO of People, you would have to go back to explain the employment brand and how the Glassdoor ratings affect that brand—hence why we need someone in HR to keep an eye on it.

What I Did Right

Now, on a more positive note, let's look at what I did right:

- I got some early wins without spending a lot of money. For example, we built the "brand book" (a standard marketing tool) to ensure a consistent end-to-end employee experience early on, and we did it internally rather than by using expensive consultants.

- I built the analytics function early and started publishing those numbers. The team built credibility by using data insights that were actionable.
- I took an iterative approach to initiatives, building proof points to earn the right to keep going.

What Can You Do Today?

Write down the elements of the CMO of People philosophy that you like and compare them to how HR currently works in your organization. Are you better able to articulate the shifts that HR should make and the payoffs for making them?

Takeaways

- The CMO of People thinks about business impact, not HR programs.
- They think about driving the business, not supporting the business.
- HR should focus on programs that enhance a predictive immersive experience, not ones that feel nice.
- The brand and the employee experience are central to the approach.
- The emphasis on brand makes it logical to put CSR, communications, and real estate/workplace services under the CMO of People.
- The dollar value of the CMO of People's impact is much larger than most business leaders suspect.
- The broad scope of the CMO of People forces them to be much more intensely collaborative with other members of the C-suite.
- CEOs "get" the term *CMO of People.*

Chapter 3
How a CMO of People Designs the End-to-End Employee Experience

In this chapter, I'll focus on how the CMO of People designs an immersive employee experience. I'll explore how a marketing mindset reveals new ways to enhance the employee experience.

Why the End-to-End Concept Is So Useful for the CMO of People

Marketing functions often talk about the "customer experience" instead of the "service we offer." Does this way of thinking bring any value to HR?

If you run a theme park, you might focus on whether the customers like the ride—after all, that is the service you are offering. You could overlook the fact that they had a miserable time in the parking lot. Disney is famous for seeing its theme parks as a complete end-to-end customer experience. It wants every aspect of the customer's experience—from parking the car, to buying a ticket, to waiting in line—to be a good one. Not all organizations see marketing from this viewpoint, but many who do dominate their niche. Starbucks, Amazon, and Disney are all good role models for understanding how a focus on the customer experience comes to life.

HR can take this idea from Marketing and apply it to the employee experience. If they do it right, they will turn the experience into a competitive weapon that will attract the best talent and get the most out of employees at work. This is a way of looking at employee experience the C-suite will relate to—it is a business strategy that drives performance.

Organizing Principles

The main organizing idea is "end-to-end"; It provides a simple way for the organization to think through the entire employee experience. The concept also quickly leads us to understand that the employee experience is not solely an HR concern—or worse, a buzz phrase that recruiting uses to pitch candidates; it is something the whole company delivers. Mapping the experience helps us break through the organizational silos that often hamper HR.

DOI 10.1515/9781547400515-003

The concept of touchpoints also complements the "end-to-end" strategy. Touchpoints ground the broad idea of an end-to-end experience with the specific moments when bringing the experience to life. A touchpoint occurs when an employee opens the employee handbook, walks into a meeting room, or receives a survey to complete. An employee's life is full of touchpoints; HR (and, more generally, all of management) must contemplate the touchpoints they are responsible for and determine how to ensure they deliver the right experience.

Each touchpoint will enhance or degrade the employment brand. It might be expedient to create an expense form that suits Accounting, even if it is difficult to fill out. However, if we see this as a touchpoint, and an unpleasant experience at that touchpoint would undermine the brand, then we might work up the discipline to fix it.

Why It's a Competitive Weapon

If the employee experience were just about making employees happy, then it would improve retention, but it wouldn't necessarily be a competitive weapon. The employment brand should include the critical values that drive performance. These values might be "competing to win" or "zero defects" or "fast to market"—there are many options; the common denominator is that they tie the brand to business results.

Consider how you should design a meeting room to make it a touchpoint that enhances the experience. We might think in terms of appropriate chairs or attractive artwork—in other words, ensure that it conveys the right image. If we want brand to be a competitive weapon, then we would also think about how to design the room to drive productivity. You've probably walked into rooms that kept you from being productive for the first ten minutes because the technology was hard to set up or the whiteboard markers had all run out of ink or the seating wasn't conducive to the brainstorming that needed to get done. We want an experience that conveys the right messages and helps the work get done. The experience should speak about your operating norms (effective management tips or product demonstrations if applicable) and culture (color schemes or signage about values). Creating this kind of experience requires collaboration between the director of employee experience and the people in Real Estate/Workplace Services, Communications, and IT.

For the CMO of People to get full value from the brand, they need to underline that it's an end-to-end experience that drives productivity and allows employees to do their best work.

What Can You Do Today?

When you walk into a meeting room in your organization, what brand messages does it intentionally or unintentionally convey? Are there any touchpoints where the employee experience prevents employees from doing their best work? Could you improve these touchpoints and use them to show people what you're trying to accomplish in building an end-to-end experience?

How to Map the Employee Experience

How we map the employee experience will guide how we design it.

The concept of the customer journey comes from Marketing. It might seem blindingly obvious to focus on customers, but compare it to Marketing's classic "product-centric" view that directs attention toward "product, price, and positioning." The customer journey concept focuses attention on the end-to-end customer experience.

Figure 3.1 shows how Marketing's idea of the customer journey *might* be applied to employees. It shows the series of steps an employee goes through from the earliest moment of a candidate's awareness of the company at the start of the recruiting process to their role as "alumnus" after they have left the company.

Let's be generous and recognize that this is a first step in the right direction. It looks holistically at employee touchpoints from start to end.

Figure 3.1: Customer journey applied to HR (traditional view)

From the perspective of a CMO of People, there is one significant shortcoming in the perspective of the journey as shown in Figure 3.1—it does not focus on the customer (i.e., employee). The steps in Figure 3.1 follow the workflows and activities of the HR department. For example, it starts with "awareness" which is where HR advertises a job, followed by a candidate "inquiry" which HR responds to, and through all the steps HR needs to bring a candidate to "offer/acceptance" and from there to HR's onboarding process right through to the time an employee exits the organization. The focus is actually HR-centric, not employee-centric. If we redo this exercise with the employee experience foremost in mind, then we end up with the customer journey shown in Figure 3.2.

Figure 3.2: Customer journey applied to HR (employee's view)

Compare the first three steps in Figure 3.1—Awareness, Inquiry, and Initial Screening—to the first three steps in Figure 3.2—Leadership, Direct Manager, and Workplace. Figure 3.1 leads HR to focus on what it must get done; Figure 3.2 leads HR to focus on the experience it must deliver. The candidate should experience the passion of leadership, the interest the direct manager shows in them, and the excitement of the workplace.

It's difficult to overestimate the importance of redrawing the customer journey. This employee-centric perspective leads to a raft of decisions, small and large, that creates an immersive employee experience.

Design Perspective

This employee journey map clearly exemplifies how the CMO of People model is rooted in design thinking. First, the experience is seen as a whole; it is an integrated offering, not a set of stand-alone processes. Secondly, it is seen from the perspective of the employee, not HR. The primary goal is not to do something that is convenient for the HR administration, but to do something that delivers the desired outcome: an exceptional employee experience that drives results.

What Can You Do Today?

Create a "back of an envelope" map that details how employees experience your organization throughout their journey. Does anything stand out as a sore point where the experience is not aligned with what you want to achieve?

The Importance of "Predictable" and "Immersive"

A CMO of People will talk about a predictable and immersive end-to-end experience that drives productivity. Those are a lot of words, but each one has a purpose.

In the previous section, I talked about an end-to-end experience that drives productivity. Now let's add in the last two concepts: *predictable* and *immersive*.

A Predictable Experience

Starbucks is the gold standard for a predictable experience. Customers can walk into a Starbucks anywhere in the world, from Beijing to Berlin, and be confident about their experience. Does your employee experience deliver the same predictability?

Predictability sets a high bar for the employee experience. Starbucks would not be satisfied with the result that "most of our stores are clean" or "our baristas are usually pleasant." They put so much effort into predictability because one bad experience can undermine dozens of good ones. Customers like to know what they'll be getting—it's no different for employees.

Since managers have a big impact on experience, it's a good idea to set expectations by orchestrating a baseline experience that managers have with new employees. The orchestration demands coordination between Recruiting,

Onboarding/Training, IT, Real Estate/Workplace Services, and the manager. The manager should see the results of this effort in its impact on making a new employee productive. Perhaps it is worth pausing to note how this focus on a predictable experience executes; it presumes an organizational culture that sees this kind of collaboration across silos as a natural way to operate.

Predictability also drives productivity. People are more effective when they know what to expect. People are more focused when they're not distracted by an inconsistent experience. I'm serious about the phrase I keep repeating: "A CMO of People architects an immersive and predictable employee experience to improve productivity and drive performance"—each word in this phrase matters.

An Immersive Experience

When Electronic Arts launched its game *Battlefield* it treated employees to an army helicopter landing on the work campus—that's a fine example of creating an immersive experience. As with "predictability," the term "immersive" is meant to raise the bar on what we expect the employee experience to deliver.

If the workplace experience is simply pleasant and generic, then it's not immersive. The goal is to go beyond employees liking the company or accepting its goals, and to get to the point where they deliver their best work because they believe in it.

To achieve an immersive experience, take care of all the touchpoints in the end-to-end employee journey and ask how to increase it a notch to create a memorable effect. You won't often have army helicopters, but the sum of everything you do should create a "wow" in employees that encourages them to feel that the company is a special place to work.

Isn't This Pretty Basic Stuff?

Helicopters aside, you might think that creating an employee experience is pretty basic stuff. That's a fair observation. There is nothing in the concept of a predictable, immersive experience that requires special skills or new technology. What's special is recognizing how taking this concept seriously will contribute to creating teams of highly productive employees. If we continue to think of the employment brand as a real factor that drives performance, and not window dressing to attract candidates, then we'll use the end-to-end experience as an organizing principle for much of what HR does.

What Can You Do Today?

Is there any aspect of your company's employee experience that has a bit of a wow-factor? One that contributes to an immersive experience? An event you run or a particular program? Find the best example and hold it up as the type of end-to-end experience you want to achieve.

How to Create the Discipline Needed to Make the End-to-End Experience a Reality

We've been looking at the concept of a predictable, immersive, end-to-end employee experience as a guiding principle for an HR function. The challenge is not so much in understanding the concept of the employee experience (i.e., the employment brand)—it's having the discipline to make it real.

The Concept Is Straightforward; Why Don't All Companies Apply It?

It's easy to see how the concept of "customer experience" translates to the idea of "employee experience." However, despite HR's focus on employees, seeing the world in terms of the employee experience doesn't come naturally. HR has heavy administrative and compliance responsibilities. When HR needs to quickly fill a lot of job vacancies, it's natural to focus on getting it done, rather than thinking about what the process feels like from the candidate's point of view. When it comes to compliance, the emphasis is on forcing employees to stay within legal and policy guidelines, rather than wondering how this links to a predictable experience. No one will disagree when you say that HR should promote a positive employee experience; however, if you are serious about making that happen, then you must recognize that this mindset does not flow easily from HR's core duties.

It's also natural for leadership to see the employee experience as "nice to have" rather than as a competitive weapon. Without creating the shared vision with your executive team colleagues, investment in the extra effort required to create a predictable, immersive experience is unlikely to be forthcoming.

Ongoing Corralling of Executives

Let's look at two components that organizations can put in place to create the necessary discipline to sustain an effective end-to-end employee experience. The first is keeping executives aligned. All executives have their own priorities; Even if they fully buy into the concept of using the end-to-end employee experience as a strategic weapon, they will always have competing priorities. The CMO of People and employee brand director must consistently act as champions for the employment brand and corral executives who over time will see a measurable difference.

In particular, the CMO of People must use data to continually articulate why the employee experience is a competitive weapon and how well the company delivers that experience.

A Rolling 18-Month Strategy

A second component for creating discipline is an 18-month rolling HR strategy that is reviewed quarterly. A longer strategy plan, such as three years, felt too long for a fast-moving business; a shorter period, such as six months, felt too short given that some of the things we wanted to do had long lead times. Each quarter, we'd review what we had achieved (looking for data to inform our judgment) and review our plans for what we needed to do in the next 18 months.

These strategy meetings ensured that we could have sustained a focus on the many different things we needed to do to sustain the brand.

Figures 3.3, 3.4, and 3.5 show how we told the story of HR strategy at Shutterfly.

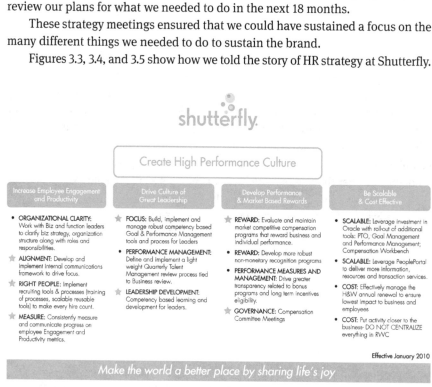

Figure 3.3: Pillars of a high-performance culture

2012-2013 HR Roadmap

COMPANY THEMES
- $1B in revenue
- Multi-brand, global operations
- Acquisitions are core to growth and winning

HR THEMES
- Great leadership bench strength across the company
- Build retention and awareness in the market
- Scale HR for a global company and workforce

Global Competitive, Engaged & Productive Organization	Leadership for Great Results	Extend Our Global Culture	Scaling HR Services
ORGANIZATIONAL CLARITY: implement and improve organizational structure that is consistent with our company-wide growth plan	**COMMUNICATION:** assure employee and manger expectations regarding the employment brand are aligned and that engagement is constantly tested and improved	**REWARDS:** provide total rewards that emphasize high performance through differentiated attraction, motivation, recognition and reward programs.	**HIGHLY SCALABLE, GLOBAL READY HR:** Deliver our new leading edge ERP solution. Deliver processes that will support, scaling to larger and/or International businesses and that support employee self service.
ALIGNMENT: drive clarity of responsibility and accountability to increase engagement and drive productivity	**EXECUTIVE INSIGHT:** deliver relevant real time insights and information regarding our employees to drive business and people decisions	**VALUES:** Focused integration of company values, emphasizing employee engagement, results and corresponding rewards.	**EVERYTHING ONLINE:** Automate execution of our HR Business processes to increase online transaction services and strengthen paperless environment
PERFORMANCE MANAGEMENT: equal focus on the "what" and the "how" to develop effective business leaders and improve productivity	**LEADERSHIP:** build enterprise flexibility by developing and strengthening our leadership bench.	**COMMUNICATIONS:** provide a global platform to drive consistent messaging for company information to increase knowledge and engagement.	**COST:** Maintain competitive health care coverage while minimizing costs
RIGHT PEOPLE: Ensure that we have the highest performers in the right jobs to maximize our business performance	**LEARNING & DEVELOPMENT:** increase engagement and retention of key employees by providing relevant learning and skill development.	**CELEBRATE:** Support activities that emphasize our employment brand of performance and fun.	**GOVERNANCE:** Maintain market-competitive and compliant compensation and benefit programs and document the HRIS processes. Provide transparency regarding costs and eligibility of base, bonus, equity & benefits
RIGHT PEOPLE: Effectively compete externally for top talent through innovative talent acquisitions, strategies and methods.	**CAREER MANAGEMENT:** maintain our high performance workplace and grow our top talent through compelling career growth opportunities	**SOCIAL RESPONSIBILITY:** Communicate and support activities that contribute to our local communities and that are aligned with our organizational values	

Make the world a better place by sharing life's joy

Figure 3.4: Roadmap showing HR's priorities

PEOPLE & PLACES | ROADMAP   SHUTTERFLY (INC)

COMPANY THEMES
- one global customer centric family of brands
- one high growth innovative business
- one results oriented $1B+ organization

PEOPLE & PLACES
- one inspiring company for all employees and candidates
- one employee brand known for leadership, innovation, results and fun
- one set of people practices focused on empowering leaders and teams

ONE COMPANY

Highly Engaged People	Great Leadership	Winning Culture	Foundation for Growth
ORGANIZATIONAL CLARITY Drive improved results through greater accountability and clarity of responsibility	**PERFORMANCE MANAGEMENT** Focus equally on the "what" and the "how" to develop effective business leaders and improve productivity	**WORKPLACE** Create a differentiated and collaborative workplace that drives productivity and a sense of pride	**RIGHT PEOPLE** Effectively compete externally for top talent acquisition strategies, practices and technologies
ALIGNMENT Communicate to current and future employees the power of INC for greater retention and higher engagement	**EXECUTIVE INSIGHT** Deliver actional real time insights regarding our employees to drive business results and people decisions	**COMMUNICATIONS** Provide a global platform for company consistent messaging for company information to increase knowledge and engagement	**READY HR** Deliver global HCM solutions to support global scaling and empowering leaders and teams
VALUES Deliberately integrate our values into all communications, rewards and recognition	**LEADERSHIP** Build engagement and retention of key employees by providing targeted learning and skill development	**CELEBRATE** Support activities that emphasize our employment brand of performance and fun	**EVERYTHING ONLINE** Automate all HR processes to drive a paperless department in order to reinvest HR resources in client facing services
RIGHT PEOPLE Ensure that we have the highest performers in the right jobs to maximize our business performance	**CAREER MANAGEMENT** Maintain our high performance workplace and grow our top talent through compelling career growth opportunities	**SOCIAL RESPONSIBILITY** Communicate and support activities that contribute to our local communities and that are aligned with our organizational values	**MANAGED COSTS** Maintain competitive health care coverage while minimizing costs; provide transparency regarding costs and eligibility of base, bonus, equity and benefits
Rewards Provide total rewards that emphasize high performances, through differentiated attraction, motivation, recognition and reward programs			**GOVERNANCE** Maintain market-competitive and compliant compensation and benefit programs

Figure 3.5: Four themes for creating success at Shutterfly

Review the processes you have in place to bring discipline to creating an immersive and predictable employee experience. Are they strong enough? If not, what can you do differently?

How to Create a Brand Book

A brand book is a crucial tool in maintaining the employment brand.

Marketing departments create brand books to help them create a consistent brand.

A brand book provides general guidelines on issues like mission, tone of voice, and the company storyline; it also provides specific guidelines on things like fonts, colors, and logo usage. No one is surprised when the CMO of Amazon, Coca Cola, or Skype produces a brand book. No one should be surprised that a CMO of People will create a brand book for the employment brand.

Here's an example from my time at DocuSign at the highest level of mission:
- *Why.* Our vision is to empower the world to keep business digital.
- *How.* Our mission is to enable anyone to transact anything, anytime, anywhere, from any device. Securely. This is how we do it.

At the more granular level, the brand book has:
- *Tone of Voice.* We are collaborative and passionate. We work as a committed team. Our voice is conversational, fun(ny), confident, and professional.
- *Color.* The DocuSign color palette features a predominantly blue scheme accented with DocuSign yellow and additional hues from our brand.

A brand book would typically be 30–100 slides long (it's more like a PowerPoint deck than a manual).

HR wouldn't normally create the employment brand book entirely on its own for a couple of reasons. First, it must align with the company's overarching corporate brand. It's a disaster waiting to happen if you let the external customer-facing brand diverge from the internal employee-facing one. If the brands diverge, sooner or later it becomes so visible that it damages both brands. Secondly, HR normally doesn't create the brand book on its own because it's a lot of work and requires skills not found in HR. Marketing could loan some of its employees to HR to help create the brand book.

An example of a brand book is shown in the Appendix.

What Can You Do Today?

Start creating a brand book that documents the rules around the end-to-end employee experience. Once you have the beginning of the brand book, use it to get executives aligned on its application across all channels. This becomes an educational process for them and you. Don't get bogged down with trying to get all the details into the brand book—just start by writing down the most important principles you want the company to follow. You'll build it from there.

How to Design the Job of Employee Brand Director

One role you'll probably need to sustain a predictive, immersive, end-to-end experience is the employee brand director. We'll look at what that role does and how to staff it.

Creating the Role of Employee Brand Director

If your organization is serious about sustaining an end-to-end experience that drives productivity, you need a person who is responsible for coordinating what happens at each touchpoint. That person is the *employee brand director*, who would report directly to the CMO of People. The employee brand director has a view across all the HR functional areas to ensure predictability of the experience through the employee's lifecycle.

Issues an Employee Brand Director Might Consider

The employee brand director would usually be working in collaboration with other leaders; often doing hands on work themselves, sometimes providing guidance to others. Here are some examples of tasks an employee brand director would be involved in:

– *Review interview questions to ensure that they align with the brand.* For example, if the brand emphasizes teamwork but the interview excludes questions about teamwork, then something is amiss. The employee brand director would identify and address the oversight.
– *Edit role descriptions to ensure that they align with the brand.* For example, if the employment brand emphasizes customer focus, then most role descriptions should include accountabilities related to serving customers.

– *Coach authors of official communications to all employees (e.g., CEO) to support the brand.* This coaching could include surface issues like font and colors, deeper issues like tone, and, most important, checking that the messaging is consistent with the brand.

The employee brand director delivers the day-to-day manifestation of the concept of a predictive, immersive experience at each employee touchpoint. It mirrors the attention to detail you would see from any fine craftsperson intent on creating a product of superior quality. If you are serious about a competition-beating employment experience, then you have to sweat the details—which means that you need someone whose job it is to sweat the details.

What Can You Do Today?

Look back at the list of three issues that an employee brand director might consider. Who is keeping an eye on those issues in your organization?

The Concept of Sustainable Foundations

All great marketing starts with a great truth about the company. Too often, companies try to communicate something they want to be or an impression they want to give. However, if you start working against truth people eventually see through it. That backfires both in terms of how customers see you and how your own employees see you.

—Brad Brooks, CEO of OneLogin, former CMO of DocuSign

The concept of building sustainable foundations is relevant to any business model, and is of special interest to the CMO of People because of how it plays out with the employment brand. Foundations are the things you need to get right before you begin to build anything substantive. In many companies, the employment brand is just a sales pitch that talent acquisition hopes will attract candidates. It often reflects what the company wishes it were like, rather than accurately saying much about what the company is truly like. In many ways, it's just a short-term tactic with no long-term or strategic significance. It's like putting up a nice looking storefront that leads into an unfinished store.

In the CMO of People model, the employment brand is, as I've said throughout this book, a competitive weapon for driving business impact. It's what brings in and keeps the best people, and it guides the creation of an environment that allows them to do their best work.

If the employment brand is to mean anything, it must be real; it must reflect how the company truly operates. If management likes the idea of being an agile company but is in fact slow and bureaucratic, then the solution is not to dress up the employment brand with false promises—the solution is to fix the actual culture.

I describe it as a "sustainable" foundation because unlike the foundation of a building which once built will last for decades, an employment brand will erode without constant maintenance. It's not enough to build great experience now; It must be an employee experience that the organization is confident it can sustain over time, through the highs and lows of the business cycle.

Starting with the truth makes for a strong and sustainable foundation. You can determine the truth by talking to employees. When the culture aligns with something you are happy to share with the outside world, then you can begin communicating your employment brand.

Sustaining Rather Than Launching

It is often a good idea to get staff focused on what is sustainable, rather than letting them fall in love with the excitement of a launch. Launching something new is fun; sustaining it over time is hard work. Continually helping staff to see their work as building foundations that need to last for many years is one way to reduce the risk of the wheels falling off as the company grows.

The employment brand can be difficult to sustain because:
- Newly hired managers might not understand the brand and may inadvertently deviate from it.
- The pressure to achieve short-term results can convince managers to short-change the brand.
- Lack of attention to the brand, once the initial launch has passed, can lead to its gradual deterioration.

Overcoming these barriers doesn't involve any special tricks—it just means that the CMO of People must make sustaining the brand a core and ongoing objective. The CEO must hold them accountable for ensuring that they don't let the employment brand degrade, just as they hold the CMO accountable for not letting the customer brand degrade.

What Can You Do Today?

Consider how much effort your organization puts into ensuring that the employment brand reflects what it is really like to work at the company.

Doing It Right the First Time versus Iterating Forward

There is tension between the idea of building foundations and quickly iterating your way forward.

It's easy to make an argument for taking the time to build sustainable foundations. It's also easy to make a case for working with what you have and quickly iterating forward. The problem arises when you notice that, by and large, these two arguments contradict one another.

The resolution lies in distinguishing between what must be done right to prevent future problems and what can be sorted out as you go along. To continue with the architecture analogy, it's self-evident that you need to get the building's foundation right even if takes much longer than expected. On the other hand, it might make sense to rush the interior paint job and furniture selection just to make it habitable and then iterate your way to what you ultimately want.

Things to Get Right the First Time

There are five things that stood out for me as CMO of People where it made sense to invest in building the foundation (i.e., to get it right the first time). The following list applies to a fast-growing technology firm, but you might find that a different list is appropriate for your situation. In any case, I focused on getting the following five things right:
1. Employment brand
2. Organization culture
3. Choice of technology infrastructure
4. Automated versus manual processes
5. The right people

I've already talked about the employment brand. You don't want to go forward with a fake employment brand because ultimately people will notice that it's false and you'll create disillusionment that is difficult to fix.

Organization culture is another thing that is easier to get right at the outset than it is to fix later. In companies where the culture is a problem, getting it sorted out should be a top priority since you won't get the full business impact from your talent if the culture gets in their way.

Within the HR organization, there were two particular norms that I emphasized from the start. One was that we would always come to the table with data. The other was that we would be 80 percent collaborative and 20 percent secretive (i.e., work had to be done behind closed doors). The emphasis on collaboration was necessary because HR usually does just the opposite—20 percent collaborative and 80 percent behind closed doors.

The choice of technology infrastructure is clearly foundational because it's going to be in place for a decade or more. In my experience, the big decision was choosing an infrastructure that far exceeded our existing needs because we were confident that we would grow into it and that the absence of this infrastructure would inhibit our growth.

Related to technology is the notion that you should get automated processes set up early on, rather than making do with manual processes with the intent to fix them later. The problem with manual HR processes in a growing company is that they end up eating up all of HR's time and it's difficult for the organization to get around to fixing them. If you know that you will be doing high-volume hiring in a few years, don't set up manual processes that can only handle low volumes— automate the processes from the start.

It's a bit of a cliché that you need to hire the right people, but it needs to be said. If you staff your company with mediocre people because it's expedient, it will drag you down for years.

Where to Iterate Your Way Forward

If you have the right foundations, then iterating your way forward with just about everything else makes sense. Analytics is one of the most important areas for iterating your way forward. If you wait until your data and analytics are perfect before presenting your findings, you'll never get anything done. Presenting numbers that you're not 100 percent sure about can be painful—however, as long as you're clear with stakeholders about the quality of the data and why it is that way, you're still better off with some preliminary data rather than no data at all.

Consider what really needs to be put right before the HR organization can move forward. Is there one area where you've been trying to iterate your way forward when you really need to shift priorities and get it sorted out now?

Making It Happen

The following tips will ensure that a sustainable foundation isn't overlooked.

There's no neat formula for avoiding the common fate of rushing ahead with what's expedient instead of building foundations, but here are a few tips.

Give it a name. The phrase "sustainable foundations" captures the idea that there are fundamentals we must get in place before we can think about frills. It is the notion that these fundamentals must be something we can and do sustain. If you make that phrase a guiding principle for the HR organization, it's more likely to be taken seriously.

Rely on your team. As an energetic CMO of People, the risk is trying to do too much yourself, at which point you get dragged into the weeds and don't have enough time for strategic issues. This is in part a question of delegation, but it's also a question of not under-hiring for positions. Don't hire people with the thought that they'll be fine because you can supervise them—hire people who are so good that they don't need your supervision.

Get in the habit of asking simple, uncomfortable questions. A lot of good management comes from the willingness to ask obvious questions that people might be avoiding because the answer will be uncomfortable. For example, asking, "Who is responsible for ensuring that will happen?" often surfaces a truth that people around the table know: the item isn't going to get done. It's better to ask the question than it is to let people pretend everything is fine.

Is there a simple question you should be asking even though the answer will likely be uncomfortable?

Outside Perspective: Gregg Gordon

An expert provides a fresh example of mapping an experience.

Gregg Gordon, author of *Your Last Differentiator: Human Capital,* sees mapping the employee experience from an Operations perspective. He notes that what Marketing would call "customer experience mapping" or HR might call "the employment journey" is similar to a tool from lean manufacturing called "value chain mapping." In all cases, the idea is to break down each step in a process and lay it out on paper so we can see what's happening from different stakeholders' perspectives.

Gordon shares an employee/manager journey map on an everyday process: dealing with an unplanned absence (Figure 3.6).

	Employee	Paper	Spreadsheet	Landline	Clock	PC	Mobile Phone	Tablet	Personal Interaction	Manager	
Stress over child and work	Awake to a sick child						(mobile)				
Stress about asking for a personal favor or incurring extra expense	Text friends and family for childcare						(mobile)				
Stress about asking for a favor	Text to try and find shift coverage on own						(mobile)				
Stress about causing a problem for the manager	"Call out" to supervisor. Leave a voicemail.			(landline)			(mobile)			Receive voicemail from employee	
Anxiety grows. Will this impact my hours for next week?						(PC)				Get list and contact info of potential substitutes	Stress builds. Will this cause OT? What if no one can cover?
									(personal interaction)	Identify someone specifically	Do they want to work or are being accommodating? What impact am I having on their personal time?
					(clock)					Adjust Schedule and/or timecard	More administrative time taken away from productive work

© Kronos Incorporated

Figure 3.6: The employee/manager journey

What leaps out from the map is that the process is neither easy nor efficient from the manager's and employee's perspectives. Not only does the experience get in the way of being productive, but it also sends the wrong brand message about "how we get things done around here."

The company Gordon works for, Kronos, builds workforce management software, and they use this kind of mapping to redesign their products. For an organization, this kind of mapping highlights problem areas they should change.

Perhaps one takeaway for the average HR manager is that while a phrase like "value chain mapping" or "employee journey mapping" may sound intimidating, the application is pretty straightforward. You can do this mapping on your own—you probably don't need a consultant with specialized skills.

Whoever in HR is running a particular process (such as dealing with absences) will know how to do all the steps. What "mapping" does is get everything down on paper in a fair amount of detail. It will often surprise the individual just how much is involved when they take the time to write it out. When it's down on paper, it's easier to see how the process might be improved.

From a CMO of People perspective, an important part of the mapping work is that it's done from the perspective of an employee working through the process, not from the perspective of HR. We want to understand how the employee experiences the process—Is it tedious? Unclear? Seemingly unnecessary?—rather than looking at the process from the viewpoint of the HR professional who is managing it.

Another takeaway from Gordon's example is that mapping the employee journey isn't something you do once and then file away. This tool, this way of thinking, pervades everything HR does and is relevant to a big-picture view of the whole employee lifecycle and also to the specific everyday actions, like calling in for a day off.

Takeaways

- The employee journey diagram outlining each step in which employees interact with HR is one of the most powerful tools for quickly conveying some of the main elements of the CMO of People approach.
- The brand book takes an abstract concept and makes it real; it also marks the intense collaboration that exists between Marketing and HR.
- Words like "predictive" and "immersive" have real meanings; they set a standard for the type of employee experience you need to create.
- The difficult part is not in the CMO of People concepts—it's in creating the discipline to apply those concepts.
- The term "sustainable foundations" is helpful in getting leaders and HR to invest in those things that will be needed in the next few years to enable the company to scale.

Chapter 4
New Points of Leverage

A CMO of People makes good use of unconventional levers.

A Non-Traditional View of HR Leverage

Leaders have a pretty good sense of how HR has traditionally had an impact on the organization. The CMO of People model asks them to look at new sources of leverage.

If you asked a typical CEO about why HR matters, they'd talk about how "recruiting is incredibly important," "training is essential," and "culture is crucial." However, framing the levers HR can push (i.e., work on recruiting, training, or culture) that way risks focusing HR on its operational silos and disconnecting it from the broader business. If HR only affects the business in traditional ways, it is unlikely the CEO will be able to make full use of HR's ability to change the company's growth trajectory.

An alternative way to look at where an HR leader can get leverage is to focus on how he or she interacts outside of the HR functional areas. How does the CHRO work with the CMO to drive business results? How does the CHRO work with the CFO to maximize revenue? How are functions like Real Estate and CSR folded into HR so that they have the maximum impact on sustainable profitability?

In this chapter, we'll look at four unconventional points of leverage:
- The relationship with the CMO
- The relationship with the CFO
- The work of Real Estate/Workplace Services
- The work of Corporate Social Responsibility (CSR)

Pragmatism over Sophistication

One surprising outcome of taking an unconventional view of how the company should deploy the HR organization is that HR might become, in a sense, less sophisticated. Let's imagine that the organization finds that breaking into a new market is much harder than expected. Tell that to a traditional talent acquisition team and they'll ask for money for more sophisticated tools for finding and

DOI 10.1515/9781547400515-004

assessing talent. The training group may ask for money for gamified, mobile, neuroscience-based learning programs. The compensation group may bring in consultants to come up with more elaborate incentive schemes. The company will end up with sophisticated recruiting, training, and compensation. It's the sort of thing that might be written up in a trade magazine, but it might not solve the problem of breaking into a new market.

If you are serious about looking for leverage outside of traditional HR specialties, and see collaboration as an action and not just a value, then when the company struggles to break into a new market, the HR executive will spend long hours with other members of the C-suite looking for the root problems and pragmatic solutions to move past the barriers. The fact that an individual function like training or compensation is doing something state-of-the-art won't have much appeal. Even it's not an HR problem—for example, the problem might be an unclear customer value proposition—HR will still be part of the top team working together on the problem, instead of retreating to their own teams.

Rather than seeking higher performance through more sophisticated and often complex programs within HR, the CMO of People seeks a pragmatic understanding of the business issues and then collaborates with the C-suite to address those issues as a team.

What Can You Do Today?

Ask yourself if your organization sees HR as disconnected specialties (e.g., training, talent acquisition, reward). Does your organization value sophisticated solutions over pragmatic ones? If so, it might be missing the boat in using HR to drive overall business outcomes.

Using the Relationship with the CMO to Get Results

For HR to drive growth in the company, it must lock arms with the CMO.

> The striking thing about Marketing and HR is how similar the roles are. Both are focused on a particular audience and how we can use the brand to influence the behavior of that audience in a manner that makes us a more successful company.
>
> —Brad Brooks, CEO of OneLogin former CMO of DocuSign

It might come as a surprise to find the HR leader listing their relationship with the CMO as a point of leverage. Normally CMOs and CHROs are friendly, but don't regularly work together. However, in the CMO of People model, HR can't get its work done without an intensely close and collaborative relationship with Marketing. How close? Brad Brooks estimated that as CMO he spent five to twenty hours a week with the head of HR.

Using the Leverage that Comes from a Strong Relationship

To execute their vision, a CMO of People needs the Marketing department's insights on the company brand, how that supports the employment brand, and vice versa. Marketing may also have specific skill sets in brand building—such as expertise with creating personas—that HR can learn from.

However, the collaboration works both ways. At DocuSign, when CMO Brad Brooks discovered that companies didn't quite understand the value of the Docu-Sign product, both in the efficiency of operations and as a way to enhance their users' experience, he held a visioning exercise to find a solution. The visioning exercise involved 55 people from across the company, and he needed HR to be a major contributor. HR was also involved in executing the steps taken to improve the customers' understanding of the value proposition. Close collaboration—which means time and effort, not a feeling of togetherness—was the normal mode of operating.

Not Everyone Buys into This Model

For years, MasterCard's Marketing department did not want HR to use their marketing brand ("Priceless") as part of their employment brand. Rather than trying to align their employment brand with their external brand, they worked to keep them separate. It's easy to understand why. Marketing considered the external brand so valuable that they felt they couldn't risk it being diluted in some way. It takes an unusually close relationship between Marketing and HR to truly collaborate on the brand. This relationship may not be a priority in most companies, but the question is whether it should be a priority in your organization.

How to Build the Collaborative Relationship

Brooks uses the phrase "trust built from shared execution." This reminds us that trust is not just a matter of goodwill; it is built when each side makes promises and then delivers on those promises. It always impressed him when HR was clear about what they would do as part of the mutual projects and how they would measure their work—and then getting those results.

We shouldn't underestimate the importance of the five to twenty hours per week that Brooks spent working with the HR executive. A deep relationship requires an investment of time.

Beyond the broad issue of trust, a CMO will only be willing to share resources with HR when it's clear that HR understands what they are trying to do and how Marketing's talent will help. It must be evident that HR is aligned with the company's goals and that the initiatives they pursue support those goals and won't end up being a distraction.

Be prepared to invest a lot of time and effort in leveraging the collaboration between Marketing and HR.

Where Do Companies Go Wrong on the Employment Brand?

If there is no close collaboration between Marketing and HR, then the external brand and employment brand can diverge. It's subtle at first, but eventually it hits a point where employees realize that their experience doesn't match what the company tells customers it stands for.

The problem often begins when the CEO is somewhat vague about the brand. As a result, HR and Marketing come up with their own interpretations. Let's not blame the CEO for this one, however—we should blame the CMO and CHRO for not seeing that they must care about what the other is communicating, since there is only one brand.

Don't let the employment brand and marketing brand go off in different directions—it's easier to prevent divergence than to fix it after it has become a problem.

Can the CMO of People Go Too Far?

An over-enthusiastic CMO of People might try to shape the external brand based on what they want the employment brand to be. Yes, there is a lot of overlap and collaboration on brand, but each side must understand the boundaries.

Brooks says that, in his experience, Marketing and HR need very specific swim lanes where each side knows the expected deliverables and purposes of its resources. For example, the CMO owns the company website. Clarity about who owns what, and what aligns with the brand, is crucial.

How do you get this clarity? You need to talk. A weekly or bimonthly communication meeting between the CMO, CMO of People, Public Relations, Investor

Relations, and Employee Communications is useful—maybe essential—to getting alignment on messaging and clarity on those swim lanes.

What Can You Do Today?

If you are a CEO, CMO, or CHRO who buys into the idea that HR must work arm-in-arm with Marketing, then you must start making that happen by building trust and understanding. As Brooks advises, trust will come from shared execution—look for a small project where HR and Marketing can collaborate to create the seeds of trust.

Using the Relationship with the CFO as a Lever

The CFO is accountable for the money; the CMO of People touches a lot of money.

In most companies, the relationship between the CFO and the head of HR is usually nothing to write home about (unless the CFO is the CHRO's boss, which is another topic). However, as soon as a CEO decides that they will use the HR role to energize growth, then the HR leader (the CMO of People) must use the relationship with the CFO as a point of leverage.

The relationship with the CFO is crucial because they control the purse strings to invest in talent management and they have the insight to put a dollar figure on talent initiatives that affect the business—such as hitting growth targets. When the CFO buys into what the CMO of People is doing, a lot gets done. When the CFO is skeptical, it creates a host of barriers.

In the next section, I'll talk specifically about the role of Real Estate. At a high level the CMO of People is deeply involved with Real Estate because it has such a significant impact on the employee experience. This puts the CMO of People in the midst of discussions about office locations, long-term leases, and expensive leasehold improvements. You can't get into those areas without a close relationship with the CFO. The CMO of People relies on the CFO for expertise on investments; the CFO relies on the CMO of People for expertise on how real estate decisions will affect employee performance and productivity. This demands a collaboration of equals, not two people working in their own teams. (You'll infer from this example that the CMO of People also needs a good relationship with the General Counsel. I won't go into that, but I'm confident that you can imagine how that would need to play out.)

The CFO must also be deeply connected to the CMO of People regarding decisions about the use of equity rewards such as stock options or restricted stock. For the CMO of People, equity rewards can be designed and deployed as an incredibly powerful tool for driving behavior, motivation, and retention. For the CFO, equity rewards constitute a major cost that must be carefully justified to skeptical investors. The CMO of People needs the CFO's involvement in anything they do with equity rewards. The CFO needs the CMO of People's expertise in designing the reward so that it will achieve its intended purpose. It's another case where, for the CMO of People to have a serious business impact, they must leverage their relationship with the CFO.

These are not the only issues where the CFO and CMO of People must work arm-in-arm. Managing healthcare costs in the U.S. is a major area of collaboration. It's up to the CMO of People to consider innovative solutions that support the employment brand while controlling costs. For example, Grand Rounds—where I work—uses innovative technology to help companies who self-insure. The algorithms match employees to the right healthcare specialists based on their symptoms, which reduces the expensive and frustrating runarounds so common in health care. Don't expect the CFO to take the lead on looking at healthcare benefit options; At the same time, don't go ahead and propose an innovative approach without having the CFO involved in the discussion.

Even something as seemingly HR-focused as providing a free cafeteria as a benefit is a place for CFO involvement because it's surprisingly expensive. If it does not drive productivity and performance, the organization should seriously consider its value and genuine contribution to the broader experience. In a sales-oriented organization, commissions are a big line item in the cost of sales—the CFO has a lot to contribute to this discussion.

What Can You Do Today?

Start by asking how the relationship between your HR executive and CFO matches this ideal. Is the organization missing an opportunity to be more effective in how it invests in people by not creating a stronger relationship between these two leaders?

Using Real Estate and Workplace Services as a Lever to Enhance the Employee Experience

> If the company is positioned as being fun and professional, but a candidate walks into the office and it's a dingy place with a crabby receptionist and bad coffee, then you've already undermined the employment brand.
>
> — Robert Teed, VP, Real Estate & Facilities, ServiceNow

The physical office has a major impact on the employee experience, so it makes sense to make Real Estate and Workplace Services part of the CMO of People's team. The goal is to ensure that every element of the physical environment supports the brand. Many details can be used to craft the employee experience in this area. It covers everything from the finishes, to artwork, to food, to furniture, to access to transit, to the overall office layout.

Getting all this right requires an unusual amount of collaboration. When Robert Teed was VP of Real Estate & Workplace Services in DocuSign, he played an important role in Marketing's rebranding exercise. Teed said, "We spent a lot of time with the overall brand team and the external agency to understand how to take the brand concept and convert it into a physical brand." He also partnered with people in Recruiting, Compensation and Benefits, and People Analytics. This investment in collaboration built a detailed and common vision of what the employment brand needed to be.

Image is a guiding principle in converting the brand to a physical environment. For example, if a brand stresses "authenticity," then the colors and finishes are probably drawn from nature. If a brand is "high-tech," then the work area probably has metal finishes and modern lighting fixtures. Electronic Arts is a good example of powerfully presenting an image. Walk into the office, and you're immediately surrounded by artwork from Electronic Arts' games. There are video games in the lounge areas and sporting facilities where you can play with a real basketball (not just a virtual one). At Electronic Arts, you are not walking into a generic workspace—you are immersed in a video game company.

Another principle is driving productivity. The point of the employee experience is to drive performance so employee services should not just be perks. Teed points out how much time can be lost if people need to drive someplace for lunch. If that's an issue, then Workplace Services could include a cafeteria, arrange for food trucks, or facilitate ordering food in. Similarly, offering concierge services such as dry cleaning is partially about making employees' lives better while remaining primarily focused on removing barriers to productivity.

Teed also spent a lot of time understanding how people collaborate—how they actually work, as opposed to how we think they should work. This led to creating a lot of fluidity in the locations people could work, breaking down cubicle walls to create a variety of work environments—including making it practical to work at home or in a local café. This required working with IT and HR on policies to remove barriers to this fluid work style.

A third principle is adopting a marketing mindset and thinking of the employee as the customer. Teed used surveys and focus groups to see the workplace through employees' eyes.

Challenges to Using this Source of Leverage

Enabling Real Estate and Workplace Services to have the full impact on the end-to-end employee experience requires breaking down some well-established silos. In most companies, HR is not normally closely tied to Workplace Services. A CMO working with a branding agency wouldn't typically think of inviting the Real Estate leader to the meeting. It's easy to see why a company would want this kind of collaboration to create a holistic, consistent approach to creating a brand, but it's not how people normally operate.

Design Perspective

It is helpful to see how the CMO of People comes at things from a design perspective. As I said in the first chapter, a design perspective:
– Approaches issues holistically
– Sees things through the eyes of the customer (i.e., the employee)

From the employee's viewpoint, there is just "an experience"; the fact that the organization believes that different aspects of that experience are the responsibility of different departments doesn't matter. That's why the points of leverage in this model are unconventional. A design perspective leads us to think of the work of the CFO, CMO, Real Estate/Workplace Services and CSR as part of a greater whole.

Furthermore, the design perspective always asks about the end result: "Does this drive productivity? Is it consistent with the immersive, predictable experience? Are we keeping it simple and focused? Are the right people doing it?"

If you're implementing this approach, then you must deal with each of the parts. However, it certainly helps if you come from a design perspective where the "employee experience" is seen as a whole and there is an evident need for integration.

What Can You Do Today?

Look around the physical environment. Is there anything that leaps out as being in conflict with the brand? If so, point it out—not so much as a problem to be fixed, but as a sign that HR is not using the required levers to create a predictable, immersive employee experience.

How CSR Strengthens an Immersive Experience

We can see how the concept of an immersive experience is executed in a CSR program.

Corporate social responsibly (CSR) programs are nice to have and often sit a little off to the side of the main business where they do good work on behalf of the company. However, in a model of HR that emphasizes an immersive employee experience, the CSR programs are folded into HR. Within a coherent HR strategy, CSR becomes a lever for driving business impact.

It makes sense to put CSR within the HR function because employees care a lot about social responsibility. A survey by Cone Communications showed that 87 percent of employees are motivated to participate in CSR programs; 74 percent said that their job is more fulfilling when they make a positive impact at work; and 51 percent even said that they won't work for a company that lacks a strong social and environmental commitment.

So here we have a lever—how do we use it?

Employee-Centered CSR

Consider these elements of DocuSign's integration of CSR with employees:
- When employees first join, as part of onboarding, two hours are spent on community giveback—for example, they could put together kits of supplies for homeless youth. This way, they may truly understand what it means to volunteer to help the community.
- Each year, employees are given three days off to focus on volunteer activities.

- Rather than having the leadership decide where employees should donate money, they encourage employees to make donations, and then leadership matches those donations.
- CSR Impact events are organized by employee volunteers in each location rather than by the central CSR function.

Individually, these tactics are nice, but collectively, they help to make doing good an integral part of the employee experience.

Salesforce 1:1:1 Model of CSR

A good example of using a CSR program to drive the employment brand is Salesforce's 1–1–1 model. The triple 1 refers to giving 1 percent of Salesforce's equity, 1 percent of Salesforce's product and 1 percent of Salesforce employees' time to social causes.

Salesforce's 1–1–1 program has helped tens of thousands of nonprofits. To give just one example, they have a Workforce Ready initiative that helps young adults develop the skills they need to enter the workforce.

The employee involvement can be skills-based (helping nonprofits with technology), volunteering (they get seven paid volunteer days), or suggesting where to donate (so that corporate philanthropy reflects employees' passions, not just those of the CEO).

This model involves employees—it makes employees proud of what they and the company do to contribute to the greater good, and its emphasis on technology is consistent with Salesforce's brand. It's a nice, integrated program that is easy to understand and appreciate.

What's really interesting, not to mention impactful, is that Salesforce liked the model so much that they've been encouraging other companies to adopt it and have even provided a platform that helps them do so. Salesforce has invested a lot of thought into this model and it's great that they are sharing their lessons learned.

Integrating CSR with Sales and Marketing

The direct involvement of employees in delivering social goods is only one part of an integrated strategy. Other initiatives include:
- Donating the DocuSign product to various nonprofits
- Aligning procurement processes with CSR—for example, by collaborating with Marketing to select a vendor to provide marketing swag that was also a social enterprise (i.e., the vendor was a social enterprise that employed people who had trouble finding work).
- The CMO integrating CSR Impact events into customer events—for example, featuring employee volunteer efforts with a nonprofit that helped disadvantaged girls get involved in scientific and technical education
- Sales always communicating the company's social impact work to customers

Again, these tactics collectively demonstrate to employees that CSR is not just window dressing—it's a way of life in their organization.

Drawing Lessons from the Philosophy Behind These Initiatives

It's easy to toss around words like "integrated," "collaborative," "strategic," and "immersive." However, when you look at this collection of activities, you see how they create an employee experience that inspires, attracts, and retains talent. It improves the company's image with clients—in fact, since bigger nonprofits are an important market segment, the donations to smaller nonprofits align with the company's sales strategy.

What Can You Do Today?

Set up a lunch with the people responsible for employee experience and CSR to brainstorm how they might work together to integrate their missions. Get them to articulate their views of the employment brand.

Lessons in Elevating the HR Function

We need to reframe the HR function if we want to elevate it.

When young HR professionals hear talk of elevating the HR function, they usually think that it means people will start listening to their advice and give them bigger budgets. In terms of enhancing HR levers, the young professional would think in terms of more sophisticated initiatives.

This chapter provides a different take on what it means to elevate the HR function. The CMO of People model elevates HR by integrating it more deeply with other functions and getting it more focused on solving business issues.

This elevation and integration of HR has its costs. Nice, tidy silos can be efficient and give everyone their own playgrounds with clear boundaries of who owns what. The collaborative CMO of People model means that more time is spent working together on issues and clarifying the swim lanes—for example, if Marketing people are working on an HR project, then it's clear who is accountable for what and what the deliverables will be.

The advantage of elevating and integrating HR goes back to the numbers shown in Section 2.3, in which I estimated that the CMO of People affects 40 to

70 percent of the company's spending. More broadly, when you look at a specific business problem, half of the solutions will likely involve HR.

A big part of reframing an elevated, integrated HR function is that the focus becomes business issues rather than excellence within each HR department. In traditional HR functions, one might strive for excellent recruitment—at face value, that seems like a great goal. However, in a better integrated HR function, the thinking might be, "We don't have a problem with recruiting store managers and full-time retail staff; It's the turnover and quality of the part-timers that is killing our productivity." In this frame, you would replace a generic "excellence in recruiting" goal with "figure out how to fix the productivity problem"—and recruiting might be a big part of that.

An "excellence" focus and a "business issue" focus do not oppose one another—in fact, they should ideally merge into a single approach. However, in practice, an HR function with a focus on excellence in each HR function will behave differently from an elevated HR function that has a general management perspective.

To maximize the benefit of the HR Executive, they must be in deep collaboration with their C-suite colleagues regularly.

The general terms "elevated," "integrated," and "collaborative" have specific implications on everyday behavior. I hope that this chapter helps to make the implications more vivid.

What Can You Do Today?

Is there any place where a part of HR is "excellent/sophisticated" and yet doesn't seem to be solving the business issues that are grinding managers down?

Takeaways

- HR gets leverage beyond the traditional specialties of recruitment, training, and so on by working more closely with other C-suite leaders on business problems and by taking on new areas like CSR/Philanthropy and Real Estate/ Workplace Services.
- The amount of time the CMO of People spends collaborating with their C-suite peers is significant; they might spend five to twenty hours a week working with the CMO.

- This way of thinking deemphasizes the ever-increasing sophistication in each HR sub-function and prioritizes a general management perspective of solving issues in the most pragmatic way.
- Building trusting, collaborative relationships takes time. It involves joint successes, creating clear "swim lanes" so that people don't get in each other's way, and making and delivering on promises. Collaboration is not a feel-good thing—it's an asset that one builds.
- The role of Corporate Social Responsibility in the employment brand does not rest on one signature initiative, but on the whole suite of things that CSR does.

Chapter 5
Why Analytics Comes First

Marketing has gone through a remarkable transition to become a function obsessed with analytics. The CMO of People model mirrors that transition. It puts analytics first so that HR can focus on affecting the business.

Why Analytics Is a Priority

Do you add analytics capability after HR is set up or does HR analytics come first?

Normally, a growth company would hire HR business partners to start getting the work done, and only later hire an analytics team to measure the work. In the CMO of People model, you would hire the analytics team early on. At DocuSign, we hired a full-time analytics person right after we had a talent acquisition team, a total rewards leader, and a technology professional online—and we would have filled the role earlier if we'd found the right person sooner.

Analytics comes first because HR can't be part of the core leadership team without having the numbers. The CMO of People can't say, "I feel that talent acquisition is going well, all things considered,"—they must have data on the recruitment pipeline. They can't say, "We have a great onboarding system"—they must have data to back this up. This need for data is no different for any other business function.

This is not to say that HR business partners are not a critical element of the HR team; however, in a new company where difficult choices need to be made about priorities, analytics comes first. As the company matures, the usual HR roles will be filled in—because analytics will have already been in place as the roles are filled, they should naturally adopt the habit of using data to support decisions. HR won't have to unlearn the old "data-free" way of operating to become analytics savvy; the new hires will grow up that way.

Key Reasons Why Analytics Comes First
Credibility, confidence, and collaboration are a powerful combination for maximizing business impact. These "three C's" are best established from a basis of facts that ultimately lead to a clear, realistic plan for the future. That's why investing early and often in a high-caliber people analytics team at any organization size can be the difference between a good HR team and an amazing one. Simply put, moving from feeling to knowing develops credibility; knowing your

DOI 10.1515/9781547400515-005

customer allows you to operate with a high degree of confidence and, concurrently, your colleagues' confidence in your service growth, leading to high-impact collaboration. Even from the most basic reporting, you can learn and make investment decisions. Remember, knowing your customer and measuring what you want to become will drive accountability and results.

In a mature company that did not have the opportunity to add analytics capability early in its history, the "analytics-first" mindset shows up as prioritizing sufficient investment in analytics that the HR side of business issues are always grounded in data. This is not about making a huge investment in advanced technology; it involves demanding that HR must come to the table with numbers—and that's a matter of both capability and culture.

In Section 2.4 on the CMO of People's priorities we introduced the concept of "measuring what you want to become" which stands in opposition to the more common practice of sharing what data you happen to have. This follows from the marketing concept of "knowing your customer." The customer for HR is the business leader—they don't particularly care about HR metrics such as how many courses were given or how many positions were filled unless it directly affects the results they're accountable for. If quality of hire metrics is important to the business, but you don't have good data, share what you have anyway. The business will be happy to have something rather than nothing, even if there is considerable uncertainty, and everyone will be motivated to improve the data collection in the years ahead.

How to Get Started on Analytics in a Growth Company

The key to getting started on analytics is being willing to present the data you have, even when it's far from perfect. It's almost always the case that some data is better than no data, and if you wait until you have the perfect analytics, it will be many years before you have anything to show the leadership team.

The people you hire to do analytics need a background in quantitative work, such as experience as a business analyst or training in economics. They don't need to be data scientists—just good with numbers.

Pointing the Analytics Team in the Right Direction

The analytics team exists to help the CMO of People make decisions and effectively tell the story of those decisions. For example, the CMO of People will be involved in decisions about where to locate new operations. You can't make those decisions without some data on, for example, the cost and availability of talent. That's where the analytics team comes in.

Imagine going into a meeting where the top team is looking at different locations and the head of HR says things like, "I believe the quality of talent is higher in location A," and "The cost of labor is bound to be much cheaper in location B," and "It'll be a longer trip to visit location C." HR can't be credible if they step through the presentation without numbers. The analytics team provides the numbers to support a sound decision as best they can, given the resources at their disposal.

There are a couple of points to note in this example. First, the analytics team isn't being asked to create a sophisticated model that will pick the best location; they are providing a mosaic of numbers that help to tell an overall story. Second, the analytics team is not off in a bubble somewhere "doing analytics"—they are by the side of the CMO of People, helping to answer an important business question.

Test and Iterate

It's natural to want to impress people with HR analytics; however, when you are starting out, that shouldn't be the goal. The idea is to get some numbers, put them out there, find out what is useful and continually improve. Especially in a young company, the feeling should be, "Look, this isn't perfect, but it's what we have. Does it help?"

Test the value of HR analytics by putting the data in front of decision-makers, and then iterate to constantly improve.

Design Perspective

In analytics, the design perspective keeps us from getting dragged into the weeds about tools or data sets to the point that we lose sight of why we are doing this. The point of analytics is to help the executives get stuff done, which means that analytics must always be focused on what they need to know to make better decisions.

For example, an analytics team will often produce data about how many people are dropping out at different stages of the funnel. You might think that I'd be thrilled with that information because the funnel is a dominant part of the napkin diagram. It told me, "Yep, a lot of people are dropping out here," but unfortunately, it gave me no idea about why or what to do. All the recruiting folks had different theories about the problem but there was no way to know what changes to prioritize.

With a design hat firmly on your head, it becomes obvious that "How many?" isn't enough—we need to know why, which means gathering information such as manager and candidate experience feedback.

This design perspective avoids the common analytics trap of producing a lot of numbers that leave managers saying, "Cool, but so what?" The design focus on the bigger picture gets us to confront the "So what?" before we begin designing data collection or reporting.

What Can You Do Today?

Ask yourself if you have the resources to go into meetings with the basic analysis required to inform a decision. If you don't, then you have a case for reallocating resources from less important work or adding resources by hiring someone to focus on this type of analytics.

An Analytics Dashboard

If analytics is just a report full of numbers, no one will care. It has to answer questions.

Let's get into some of the specifics of what a talent analytics dashboard looks like. Figure 5.1 provides a full view of the talent analytics dashboard. Here are some essential dashboard design elements:

- The first thing to notice is that it uses the end-to-end employee experience as an organizing principle: it starts with the "top of the funnel" where talent is brought into the company, then into the cycle of learning, performing, being rewarded, and so on.
- Second, it is all pointed toward business impact metrics. As I said in the introduction, the CMO of People has shared accountability for business outcomes. An HR dashboard that doesn't include business measures would be misguided.
- Finally, the dashboard is organized around questions, not metrics. The questions arise from a discussion about the important things a manager needs to know instead of the usual approach of gathering a lot of numbers and hoping that something a manager needs to know is buried somewhere within them.

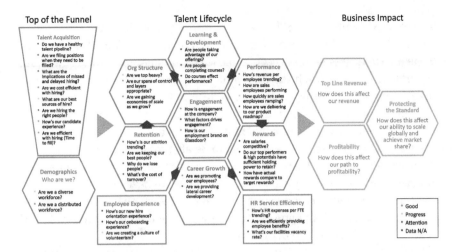

Figure 5.1: Talent analytics dashboard

Now let's take a more careful look at what is in this dashboard. Figures 5.2 to 5.4 show the individual pieces so that you can study these in more detail. Let's start with the "Top of the Funnel" in Figure 5.2. and work our way through the dashboard.

Top of the Funnel

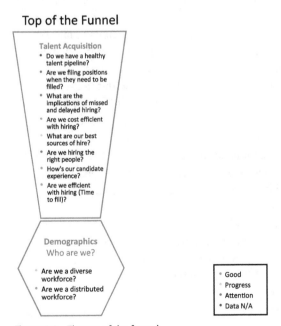

Figure 5.2: The top of the funnel

When we talk about the talent funnel, we're talking about how one starts with a broad pool of possible candidates for a job and then slowly funnels them down from many applicants to a long list of screened candidates, to a short list we want to interview, until we reach the final individual hire. It is very similar to what marketing does in acquiring customers.

In the domain of the talent acquisition function, one of the first questions we ask is "Do we have a healthy talent pipeline?" That's a broad question, but it focuses on whether or not we're going to be able to meet the talent needs of a growing organization. There's no single number that answers that question; fundamentally, we want to track how many people we have at each stage of the funnel and from there assess whether we are confident that we have enough people coming through the process that we will have the right number of good quality candidates at the end of the day.

The next question is "Are we filling positions when they need to be filled?" This relates to the more common metric of "time to fill," which tracks how long it takes us to fill a position from the time a requisition is given, to talent acquisition, to the time someone is on the job. But the question here isn't focused on the talent acquisition process—the question is about the business need and so it comes down to this: Given the needs of the business, is talent acquisition meeting these needs? Of course, one of the elements of meeting this need is how long it takes to fill a position, but that's only meaningful in relation to when they need to be filled; if the job is filled quickly but still not quick enough, we have a problem.

Next, take a look at this question: "What are the implications of missed and delayed hiring?" This is very much a business question, not a question about HR processes. The reason we're asking this is that if the implications are small we won't invest unduly in fixing them. Imagine a retail store with ten cashiers and we're short one. Yes, delayed hiring has left a vacancy, but it won't have a big impact on the store. On the other hand, if you have a new product coming off the production line and it can't be shipped for lack of a quality assurance expert, then that begins to have serious implications for the business. With this kind of question, you answer it in a more subjective or qualitative way than you would with some other metrics. That shouldn't prevent us from asking the question, because a subjective answer is better than no answer.

The next question is "Are we cost-efficient with hiring?" This is similar to the traditional "cost per hire" metric, but again notice there's a different angle on this—that difference helps illustrate how a businessperson thinks versus how, perhaps, HR is taught in colleges. What we really want to know is whether we're being efficient with the money we're spending, which is not the same as spending as little as possible. It's about making the best use of that money to get the business results we need.

Then we move to the question, "What are our best sources of hire?" which is a classic talent acquisition metric. It can be trickier to answer than you might think because sometimes candidates use several different sources of hire before they end up on your doorstep. Nonetheless, if a candidate is using several different job boards, you want to know which ones are most effective; if a potential hire is looking at campus recruiting rather than a job fair, again, you want to know which method is delivering the best talent in the most efficient way.

Next, rather than using the common metric of "quality of hire," we reframe that more broadly as "Are we hiring the right people?" which, again, is a subjective question. Part of the answer will come from discussing with managers whether we're bringing in the quality of people they need, and it also can extend into other questions. For example, perhaps we hired someone who met the job specification but in fact that job specification wasn't really what the organization needed—that means we weren't hiring the right people. All of this gets bundled into that broad question.

We then ask, "How is our candidate experience?" As I've explained, the employee experience—which we extend to include prospective employees—is a critical part of getting the best performance out of an organization, so we measure candidate experience at various stages in the process. With these measures, not only do we know if their experiences match what we want to deliver, but if they are falling short we also know where they are falling short—thus, we can take action to fix them.

And the final question in this series is "Are we efficient with hiring?" which in this case was how long it took to fill jobs (i.e., the classic "time to fill" measure).

In the "Demographics" hexagon below the Funnel questions, we have some traditional contextual information about whether we are meeting our diversity goals and a look at how employees are distributed regionally. Leaders need this contextual information to keep a clear picture of the company at the current state, which is particularly important in rapidly growing global companies where you may find things change quickly. For example, at DocuSign we went from what was a predominantly US workforce to a global workforce, and sometimes managers needed the dashboard to remind them just how much had changed.

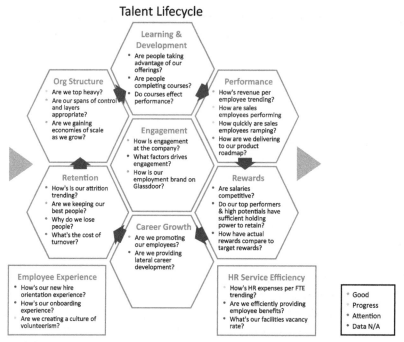

Figure 5.3: The talent lifecycle

The talent lifecycle metrics as shown in Figure 5.3 are divided into some of the major areas of responsibility within HR: learning and development, performance, rewards, career growth, retention, the organizational structure, and, at the center of it all, engagement as a unifying goal. I won't walk through each and every one of these questions, but we'll discuss many of them so you can get a sense of the thinking that led to the dashboard.

If we look at "Learning and Development," you'll want to begin with the basics of just knowing whether you are actually successfully completing the core activities. Are people taking the courses and completing them? That basic information is easily tracked. At a deeper level, we asked, "Do the courses affect performance?" Now this is a notoriously hard question to answer, but it is of course the most important question of all—so it goes on the dashboard even if at times we struggle to answer it. We want to become an organization where we're clear about how courses affect performance, and in the absence of hard numbers, we can collect subjective data from managers, employees, and trainers. We're looking for clues that there's a link between the training employees get and their subsequent performance.

In the "Performance" hexagon you'll see that the focus is on revenue and sales. That focus contrasts what you'd normally see in an HR dashboard on performance management, where the questions are usually operation metrics such as how many people have completed their performance appraisal forms. What we're capturing with these questions is what is most important to the CEO at that point in time. You'll notice the question, "How are we delivering to our product roadmap?" is one that falls completely outside of normal HR and the answer would be found in some other department. Yet ultimately the point of performance management is business results such as hitting those deadlines, so that's what we focus on in the dashboard.

With "Rewards," we start with the basics of "Are salaries competitive?" That's something we need to know, and we get that by looking at salary surveys. With the next question you can see that we're very interested in how top performers and high potentials are being retained; we're zooming in on what's most important to the organization. The final question in the set has to do with the discipline of the reward process. You may find in many organizations that there is a policy for giving merit increases and then when you look at the results at the end of the year, somehow the actual amount distribution of increases doesn't match was planned. Asking, "How have actual rewards compared to target rewards?" is a simple check on whether we're doing what we say we intended to do.

Career growth looks at the usual mobility questions about whether we are moving our employees laterally. Those metrics are easy to gather but notice how the questions are phrased in everyday language that a manager would recognize, not in terms of the HR concept of "mobility," which perhaps disguises what people actually care about.

Next, let's consider what we we're interested in when it comes to retention. First, we look at how our attrition is trending. What's interesting here is that often, managers are less interested in the absolute number than the trend; if that's what managers are using to make a decision about whether they need to take action on attrition, that's the number we're going to give them. We follow that by asking the crucial question, which is not so much how many people are leaving, but whether we are keeping our best people. We moved from there to asking why we lose people. We'll get part of the answer to that question from exit interviews. Finally, we ask what attrition is costing us. Here, we want to be truly business-savvy about how we make that estimate—not just come up with the highest number we can think of, which is often seen in HR textbooks. We want to truly understand where turnover is hurting the business, or if it is hurting the business at all.

The set of questions on "Organization Structure" reflects the issues that a growing company of our size was likely to face. One concern is becoming top-heavy—having too many managers and not enough workers. You can just potentially eyeball the answer by looking at an organization chart, or else use numbers of senior, mid-level, and junior staff. However, imagine if you just presented a table of numbers of staff by grade level—that wouldn't mean much to managers. We need to frame it as the business question of whether we're top-heavy, and then everybody will know why they're looking at the data. Just as being top-heavy is a common problem; when the organization is changing rapidly, spans of control can become too narrow or too wide, and it's easy to add too many layers or to have a layer missing. For the dashboard, it is less a matter of just producing numbers as it is focusing people on the important questions. Finally, the dashboard asks if we are gaining economies of scale as we grow, which is an issue that can plague a young, growing organization.

For the final, central hexagon, "Engagement," we asked the obvious questions of what engagement is and what drives it, and then we turn to look at engagement from outside the company by seeing what it says on Glassdoor.com.

We have also a couple of boxes at the bottom of this series of hexagons to capture some important things, such as looking at the employee experience and HR service efficiency more closely. For employee experience, we look at orientation and onboarding. We also have a metric on something important to the CMO of People model: We believe the CSR activities are an important part of the company culture and we want to be sure that we're creating that culture of volunteerism that is part of the brand promise we make to ourselves and to our employees.

Under "HR Service Efficiency," we have an element the CFO would want to know, which is how our HR expenses are trending relative to the number of employees. Again, notice that the trend is more important than the absolute number. Next, because employee benefits are a big expense, we want any insights on whether that money is being used efficiently. Finally, something else you normally wouldn't see in an HR dashboard is some data about the efficient use of facilities; this reflects the fact that in the CMO of People model, facilities fall under HR.

Figure 5.4: The business impact

The business impact hexagons at end of the dashboard, as shown in Figure 5.4, get right to the point of HR. The point of HR is not to perform a series of activities—it's not even to do things like drive employee engagement. Ultimately, the point of HR is to have an impact on the business. Whether or not it is easy to answer these questions on the dashboard, these are some of the most important questions for HR and should be prominent as part of the normal reporting activities. All of these questions on business impact will be answered in a partly subjective way, which is fine.

Just to round out this explanation of the dashboard, we use the common coloring scheme of red, yellow, and green so that we can highlight any areas where there are problems. Notice the addition of a fourth color, blue, for data not available. The use of this fourth color is to encourage us to ask the right questions even if we're not currently in a position to answer those questions with any confidence.

How We Used the Dashboard

As head of HR, I spent what might seem like an inordinate amount of time with the dashboard; that's because it was a key tool for quickly grounding discussions in fact. For example, a question like, "How does this affect top-line revenue?" would quickly move discussions away from secondary matters and focus attention on the issues that were driving business success.

The dashboard also enabled me to hold my team accountable. For example, starting at the top-left of the dashboard, I'd want to see evidence that my team had built a healthy talent pipeline. The team knew I'd be looking at this, and they'd know I'd be reviewing data, not just looking for overall assurances.

More often than not, trends mattered most to us. The trends told us if something needed to be changed and helped us to predict outcomes.

Going from the Initial Dashboard to a More Advanced Version

There is no magic measuring stick behind the questions in a dashboard. For a question like, "Do we have a healthy talent pipeline?" we'd look at data, such as the number of candidates at each step in the talent pipeline for various departments (e.g., Sales, Engineering). We'd then make a judgment as to whether it looked healthy or not.

When you start out on a dashboard, there will be missing data, inaccurate data, and data that, while correct, is misleading. The trick is to have the courage to get the data you have in front of people and start making judgments on what it means. Over time, you test, iterate, and get better—although you'll never get to the point where you can dispense with judgment in interpreting the data.

A more advanced dashboard begins to look at linkages between different types of data. For example, in an early dashboard, you might have data about how often managers are having coaching conversations with employees, as well as data about on-time delivery of projects. In a more advanced dashboard, you might present data that shows whether there is a relationship between more coaching and better on-time performance.

There are many analyses you can do—however, as a rule, look for analyses that answer a specific question, such as, "Is this activity delivering the result we want?" or, "If we want more of this, what will get us there?" An early dashboard that shows how long it takes for someone to get through the hiring process is *somewhat* interesting, but an analysis that shows whether a long hiring process causes good candidates to drop out is *very* interesting.

What Can You Do Today?

Take an existing HR report and write out three or four questions that you wish the report would answer. What would it take to redesign the report so that it did a better job of answering those questions?

Top-of-Funnel Analytics for Talent Acquisition

Here's how we use analytics for talent acquisition.

In rapidly growing firms, the top HR priorities are talent acquisition and onboarding. As a result, in the early days of a new firm, the analytics team will focus on those two areas.

Strategic Question 1: How Can I Prevent Bottlenecks in the Hiring Process?

In the firms where I led HR, an early issue was preventing bottlenecks in the hiring process. For example, we had a lot of candidates pre-screened, but the process was still held up because hiring managers were slow to schedule interviews. We looked at the hiring process in the same way that Sales looked at the selling process: It starts at the top of the funnel with prospects, and then looks at each step of the funnel until the time the deal is closed.

We'd look at where we were at each step in the funnel (e.g., how many applicants we had for a given job requisition, how many interviews had been scheduled, and how many candidates completed interviews). This let us know if there were any bottlenecks that prevented filling vacancies at the necessary rate.

We measured how long each step took. This let us know when we could expect to have vacancies filled and hence give managers reasonable forecasts on when they'd have their staffing needs met.

Strategic Question 2: How Can I Increase the Efficiency of the Hiring Process?

We also tracked the efficiency of each stage of the hiring process. How many applicants would we get from a particular source? How many applicants would make it through pre-screening? How many candidates would accept an offer? How many job requisitions could a recruiter fill?

By monitoring these metrics, we could see if parts of the process were inefficient. For example, if a job advertisement pulled in a lot of applicants, very few of whom made it through the initial screening, then it was probably not a very good advertisement. We could then continually improve the process.

Strategic Question 3: How Quickly Is the Sales Team Ramping Up Sales?

A growing firm doesn't care only about how long it takes to fill vacancies, but it also cares about how long it takes people to get up to speed. In the firms I worked with, there was a particular interest in how quickly sales representatives could get to the point that they could hit their quotas.

This analysis enabled the business to accurately forecast revenue by looking at how quickly talent acquisition could fill sales rep jobs and how quickly they could become fully productive.

Notice that this question involved Sales and HR. Doing this analysis required partnership. It reflected the mindset that we were never doing "HR analytics"—we were always doing "business analytics," which would often involve partnering with other departments.

What Can You Do Today?

Instead of thinking about what metrics to monitor, determine what business issues matter most to the organization right now. In fast-growing firms, analytics focuses primarily on talent acquisition; you might have a different business priority. Since analytics talent is a scarce resource, you must be confident that you have them working on the right strategic questions.

Lifecycle Analytics for Brand and a Predictive, Immersive Experience

> The main goal in assessing the brand is to move toward a data-based assessment as opposed to relying on anecdote or gut-feel.
>
> — Brad Brooks, CEO of OneLogin former CMO of DocuSign

Two of the most important questions we asked employees about their experience were:
- Does the workplace enable you to perform at a higher level?
- Do you feel inspired by the workplace?

Notice that the questions are not primarily about employee satisfaction. The first question concerns productivity. Remember that the whole point of the CMO of People model is to outperform the competition though superior talent management. If employees feel that the workplace isn't enabling them to perform at a higher level, then the employee experience isn't delivering what it needs to. The second question sets a similarly high goal—it's not about having satisfied (or even very satisfied) employees. It's about whether the environment inspires them to do their best work.

For example, at Shutterfly, we had a 300,000-square-foot manufacturing facility for production of cards, photoshoots, etc. It was tempting to save money by making this a bare-bones location. However, that wouldn't have been consistent with the brand. We decided to make the workplace mirror the look and feel of the corporate office as much as possible and bring to life the mission of bringing joy into people's lives. Engagement and productivity data reinforced the wisdom of this decision, because as good as data is, nothing beats a good anecdote. One Christmas season, a plant manager realized that some photo gifts wouldn't make it to a customer in time for Christmas, so the manager drove to the customers house to make a personal delivery. If the company lives the brand, then so will employees.

One time at DocuSign we experienced a low engagement result related to employee enablement and access to information, which drove the immediate decision to invest in the infrastructure to scale knowledge management. One time at DocuSign, we got shockingly bad data from employees regarding whether they could perform at a higher level. It turned out that, due to rapid growth, we'd hit a point where people couldn't find the information they needed. The informal processes for finding information weren't working, so we built an intranet site to create a scalable solution for all employees. This is not a dramatic story, but it simply shows how a commitment to gathering data leads to action that improves productivity.

Other Metrics Used to Assess the Employee Experience

We used metrics at every stage of the end-to-end employee experience. For example:

- *Candidate experience questionnaire.* Get candidate feedback on their experience applying for a job.
- *Close rates.* What percentage of job offers are accepted?
- *Net Promoter Score.* This answers the question, "Would you recommend the company to a friend?"
- *Turnover.* What is the turnover rate and how does it compare to the industry average?

As always, with metrics we are not looking for simple answers—we are trying to paint a picture that will let us know if we are on track with creating an effective experience. If we're not, then we'll dig deeper to see what we have to fix.

It's tempting to hope that one metric will reliably tell us the health of the brand. It's unlikely that one such metric exists; we are usually better off assembling a mosaic of measures that builds a picture of how the brand is doing and what we need to work on.

Greenhouse's Candidate Experience Questions

I have used Greenhouse recruiting software and they've given me permission to share the questions they use to assess their candidates' experience. They focus on their NPS (Net Promoter Score) result, which is, "Overall, my interview experience was a positive one." This answer summarizes the experience in an overarching way.

Using a "Likert" scale, they ask these three questions (which are asked in the form of a statement for respondents to agree or disagree with) that impact the net promoter score:

Do you agree with the following statements?
- I was treated with courtesy and respect.
- Overall, I have a more positive impression of the company having gone through their recruiting process.
- The interviewer(s) got an accurate sense of my strengths and weaknesses.

Additional topics we'd recommend asking in candidate survey questions are:
- Were things on time, organized, and professional?
- What are the candidate's feelings about the actual experience?
- How well does the candidate understand the role and the organization?

Greenhouse thinks a lot about how companies can improve hiring outcomes, and measuring candidate experience is a part of that.

Note that these questions are straightforward. There is very little in HR that is technically very difficult. The issue is whether or not HR cares enough about the candidate experience to ask the obvious questions and then to act if the candidate experience was not a good one.

In terms of the employment brand, some useful metrics include:

- *Employee Net Promoter Score (eNPS)*. The metric in its simplest form is the answer to one question: "Would you recommend this company to a friend?" It's a clear, simple metric that captures a lot about what employees think of the company.
- *Number of employee referrals*. The number of employee referrals is a difficult metric that complements the Net Promoter Score. It can be seen as the answer to, "Did you actually recommend this company to a friend?" which is a step up from "Would you. . .?"
- *Engagement metrics*. Employee surveys often deliver a single engagement number, but they also have many sub-factors that allow you to understand why engagement is what it is. These sub-factors are useful for assessing the effectiveness of the brand.
- *Exit surveys*. The exit surveys provide insight into what, if anything, is amiss. Usually, the trends matter more than the specific points of data, and collectively they inform management if things are on track or if something needs to change.

It is not that the metrics are remarkable—what matters is using as many of them as you can, taking seriously what they indicate, and then acting on them.

What to Aim for in an Exit Survey

Ah, the elusive exit survey. Important as it is, it's a piece of the puzzle, not the whole picture. Most exit interview processes or questionnaires aren't unique, yet the company's culture of openness and welcoming feedback will be factors in the degree of honesty a departing employee has. As the CMO of People focuses on enabling credible, genuine communications and demonstrated bias for action, the odds of more valuable, productive insights increase. Pair those insights with a leader's ability to recruit new talent, along with their engagement results, turnover statistics, promotion rates, and so on, and you begin to get a more complete picture of a leader's effectiveness.

Marketing Parallels

Measuring employment brand is very similar to what marketers call "brand-tracking." Brand-tracking looks at a mosaic of metrics that are relevant to understanding how the brand is doing. For example, brand-tracking might measure factors such as:

- Brand awareness (e.g., Do customers recognize the brand? Do they recall it when it's mentioned?)
- Brand usage (e.g., frequency of purchase; future purchase intent)
- Brand image (e.g., what consumers think about the features)

Pull all these together, and a company can make informed decisions on what it needs to do to strengthen the brand.

A small company might capture just a few brand metrics a few times a year while a large company might constantly track a large number of different measures. It's a matter of doing what's practical for the situation. The same thinking applies to measuring employment brand. You should gather as much data as you reasonably can; however, if you can't get a lot, then, as Brad Brooks says at the start of this section, anything that moves you from the world of anecdote and gut-feeling to data is a good thing.

Frequency

DocuSign looked at employment brand numbers quarterly (with the exception of the employee survey data, which was annual). That is likely a good cadence for most firms. The numbers don't change so quickly that there's a need to do it more than quarterly—however, if something is going wrong with the brand, you don't want to wait a year to find out.

An Illustration

It's not the individual metrics that tell the story—it's what a group of metrics collectively implies. For example, I worked in one organization where we noticed that in Engineering, the length of time to close a job offer was trending up, attrition was increasing, leadership ratings were falling, and referral rates were low. We might have explained away any one of those metrics, but as a mosaic they painted a picture that the employee experience wasn't what it should be. Further investigation showed that engineers were burdened with too many menial tasks. We were able to outsource those tasks, which made sense immediately in terms of improving engineering productivity, and in the long run brought the employee experience back to where it needed to be.

Find out what metrics you are using to track employment brand and the employee experience, as well as how often they are reviewed. See if someone can remember a time when they used the insights from brand-tracking to make an important change.

Lifecycle Analytics for Corporate Social Responsibility

How does HR assess the effectiveness of the investment in corporate social responsibility?

Corporate Social Responsibility (CSR) is important to both the customer brand and the employment brand. How can you use data to track how well you are doing and to illuminate where you need to make changes?

Amy Skeeters-Behrens, Executive Director of Philanthropy at DocuSign, built the CSR program around three pillars: employee donations, employee volunteering, and product donations. To see if these programs were on track, she gathered data on the following:
1. Employee donations
    o   Percentage of employees requesting matching donations
    o   Which causes employees donated to

This showed if the matched donations program was popular. If it wasn't popular, then it would need to be changed or cancelled. It also showed which causes mattered most to employees, which informed where additional direct donations might be made, or what other CSR activities they could do to support these causes.
2. Employee volunteering
    o   Percentage of employees who participate in using volunteer time

If the percentage of employees volunteering started declining, then that would be a signal that the program might be in trouble and something would have to change or that for whatever reason the employees cannot afford to take the time.

3. Product donations to nonprofits
   o Number of nonprofits who were part of the donation program that were using DocuSign
   o How extensively the product was used at these nonprofits, which would eventually give data on hours saved, water saved, and trees saved

Again, these metrics answer the fundamental question as to whether the donation program is on track. If numbers were low or trending in the wrong direction, then the company would take action. In the absence of data, it would be too easy to continue with the program because it was good in principle, or to cancel the program because no one was sure it was working.

One of the most revealing pieces of data was more qualitative than quantitative. On the employee survey, employees were given a chance to single out initiatives they were particularly happy with, and one of the most common comments was Employee Impact Events (the volunteer events designed to deliver a social good). This data point helped the organization to infer that the CSR efforts were indeed helping to enhance the employment brand.

What Can You Do Today?

Find out what metrics you are using to track corporate social responsibility programs and how often they are reviewed. See if someone can remember a time when they used the insights from the data to make an important change.

Lifecycle Analytics for Real Estate and Workplace Services

If the CMO of People function includes Real Estate and Workplace Services, then it needs analytics to underpin decisions made in these areas.

Real Estate and Workplace Services (e.g., onsite cafes, concierge services) are one element of the employment brand that drives productivity. Here are some examples of how analytics can guide the management of this function.

Workplace Services

One set of decisions focuses on what Workplace Services has to offer. There are several sources of data that help to inform those decisions:

- Survey employees on their wants and needs
- Run employee focus groups
- Get demographic data on your employee population
- Gather data on what competitors are offering

You can use a marketing technique called *conjoint analysis* that helps to rank employee preferences in a systematic way, but even if you don't do that, getting data will lead to better decisions than doing it based on gut-feel.

How Do You Do Conjoint Analysis?

The simple answer to, "How do you do conjoint analysis?" is that you don't—you hire a consultant to do it for you. Freelancers with expertise in this technique can be found on Upwork, and the major consultancies like Willis Tower Watson are experienced with doing this analysis. What will they do? They'll ask a sample of employees to choose between a number of similar sets of options—for example, choosing between a benefits package with more vacation, less pension, but no dental care versus one with fewer vacation days, the same pension, and dental care. If you found that the options with more vacations were generally preferred, then you could conclude that was a priority for employees. Of course, you wouldn't do that by eyeballing the data—there are particular mathematical techniques for determining the order of preferences based on the sets of options employees preferred.

Real Estate

Real Estate is such a big cost (perhaps 3 to 4 percent of revenue, depending on the business) that the CFO will want to keep a close eye on the expense. This attention from the CFO drives us toward financial ratios such as:
- Real Estate cost/seat
- Real Estate expense/revenue
- Seats occupied/maximum possible occupancy
- Food and beverage costs per location and per employee (driving consistent experience)

These ratios help the company to answer the question, "Are our Real Estate costs under control?" Unfortunately, these ratios can create pressure to constantly reduce costs, and if cost reduction goes too far, it can end up damaging the employee experience. Unfortunately, there is not a simple set of countervailing metrics that shows the value being realized from the investment. In lieu of countervailing metrics, the CMO of People must pull together the story, illustrating how Real Estate plays a role in the employment brand, which reduces attrition costs and increases employee productivity.

Another critical question is, "How much real estate will we need?" This is answered by classic workforce planning analytics that forecast how many and what types of jobs will be added in the near future.

Measuring Results

It would be ideal to assess investments in Real Estate and Workplace Services by directly measuring their impact on productivity. However, a team of academics would find this kind of study challenging, and it's beyond the realm of most businesses. Instead, you can measure a range of other factors that would keep your thinking grounded in data.

Indirect measures of effectiveness of the investment in Real Estate and Workplace Services include:
- Engagement and attrition
- Employee satisfaction with Real Estate and Workplace Services
- Social responsibility measures like electricity usage and LEED certification

Real Estate and Workplace Services are just two elements of the many things that affect engagement and attrition; however, if they are trending in the wrong direction, one should look at the possible causes, some of which might be in these areas.

Employee satisfaction is a more direct measure of how well Real Estate and Workplace Services are affecting the brand. It's part of the mosaic of measures that informs us as to whether we are on track.

Social responsibility measures are included because they are part of the employment brand. Including these measures follows naturally from the CMO of People philosophy of looking holistically at the employee experience. When we talk about a predictive, immersive, end-to-end experience, these are not just words—they show up concretely in everything we do, including how we do Real Estate and Workplace Services analytics.

What Can You Do Today?

There is a risk of liking all the examples in this chapter and asking your analytics team to produce all of them. What you can do today is step back and think strategically. Gather your team and ask, "If we only had time to produce a couple of the metrics discussed here, what would they be?" The answers will reveal what is top of mind with the team, and you should look to see if what the team thinks is important aligns with the organization's strategy.

Business Impact Analytics about Impact, Efficiency, and ROI

Ultimately, all the work of HR should show up in business impact metrics.

What does the CEO want to know about each of the major functions? One way to frame it is that they are looking for insights on these three issues:
- The impact of the work
- The efficiency of the team
- The overall ROI on projects

What HR needs from its own analytics team is relevant data that helps answers these questions in a timely way. The intent shouldn't be to impress the leadership with sophisticated analysis or to overplay the certainty of the data. It's that sense of, "Here is what we know, and it leads us to think this way, so this is where we are going to focus attention."

The Impact of HR Work

A good example of reporting on work impact is sharing basic recruiting metrics for each department. A department leader's own success depends on the recruiting function doing a good job, so the leader should want to know how the hiring process is proceeding (e.g., number of applications received, number of qualified candidates). That means sharing the basic data in a transparent way. The news might not always be good, but at least it's clear what HR is doing—that clarity is based on data.

A positive side effect of sharing data is that it sets up two-way communication so that HR (in this example, talent acquisition) is clearer about priorities and why it's doing what it's doing. Left in a silo, Recruiting can begin to feel that it's just going through the administrative process of filling job requisitions. Better communication reminds them that they're meeting needs that are important to business results. This communication also clarifies priorities so that as the business leaders review the metrics, they can point recruiters toward issues that have the largest or most immediate impact on results.

The Efficiency of Your Team

If other leaders first want to know what HR is getting done (the impact), then the second thing is how efficiently HR is doing it. While the HR function will want detailed measures of its own efficiency (e.g., cost per hire), then the CEO won't want those details on process efficiency—they will be interested in a broad measure such as total HR expense as percent of revenue. As with most metrics, they will be less interested in the absolute number than the trend: is it going up or going down?

CEOs monitor HR expense and total revenue because bloat is a common organizational disease. Every department wants more investment and every manager wants more staff. If leaders don't make a specific effort to combat bloat, then expenses will grow faster than revenue.

If HR expense is going up as a percent of revenue, that's a warning sign. However, there are times when it's not a bad thing. For example, a growing firm might make extra investments in HR capacity to enable the company to scale. This broad measure of efficiency, which is a simple transparent number, helps leadership to stay on top of what's going on. They then use their judgment about whether the number is appropriate given the situation.

Overall ROI of a Project

ROI can be a real challenge for HR as it attempts to justify various programs. Any truly strategic HR function, such as the CMO of People model, doesn't view the world primarily through the lens of HR programs that need to be justified—it views the world through the lens of business results that must be achieved.

For example, consider the return on an investment of a new office in Dublin. HR is part of the team behind the decision to locate a new office, so the overall ROI of this project is relevant to understanding if HR is delivering what is required.

In this case, HR was directly involved in the decision to place a new office, along with Sales and Finance. It was a partnership. Together, the team looked at issues like the availability of talent, taxation, geographical coverage of key markets, and so on. This mosaic of data led to an informed decision about where to open the office based on Financial, Human Resources, and Sales considerations.

Evidence that it was a good decision shows up in metrics like higher total revenue and higher revenue per employee—the company cared about this complete result. We didn't attempt to isolate the ROI of HR's role in the project—we just looked at overall ROI.

Another example of judging overall ROI can be found in talent acquisition. Rather than looking at efficiency measures, such as how long it takes to fill a vacancy, we can look at financially relevant issues such as, "Did the talent acquisition function fill sales jobs in a manner that led to hitting revenue targets?" or, "Did it fill engineering jobs in a manner that led to hitting project deadlines?" You can put a dollar value on it by estimating the lost revenue of projects being late. It shifts the focus from looking internally at HR processes to looking at the overall financial impact of the outcome.

HR might object that it doesn't control everything that goes into hitting a project deadline, but that measure matters most to the business, so that's where the focus should be. The "overall ROI" mindset stresses collaboration.

What Can You Do Today?

Start with the "impact of the HR work" category. Is data from talent acquisition or training being shared with the business in such a way that both HR and the business can see the impact of that work on results?

Outside Perspective: David Green

An analytics thought leader's views.

A Culture of Analytics

David Green, a widely recognized speaker, consultant and commentator on people analytics, points out that having a "culture of analytics" is more important than the tools you happen to have available. Building that culture can be a challenge since the legacy of HR has not been data-centric. One of the important steps in building that culture is to ensure there is not a big divide between the analytics team and the rest of HR. One can't presume that good two-way communication will happen naturally—an analytics pro may tend toward being a numbers-geek while a traditional HR pro may be numbers-shy. The head of HR needs to bridge that gap and avoid the trap of an us-versus-them mentality between the analytics team and the rest of HR.

Green says that one way to build the connection is to start by bringing a set of your more data-savvy HR pros into the analytics tent early. There are always a group of HR pros who are early fans of using data, either because of their own interests or because they recognize it will be good for their careers. If you make them part of the analytics effort early, they'll become advocates and will be role models who demonstrate the practical ways an average HR pro can use analytics on the job.

Creating a culture of analytics seemed relatively easy in this book because you had a data-savvy HR leader who brought analytics into the function in the early stages of the growth of the team. For more established companies, you'll need to provide the HR team with training, enable them with tools, and promote knowledge sharing through mechanisms like a community of practice.

How to Hire Data-Savvy HR Pros

Green reminds us that the transition to an analytics-savvy culture is easier if you make a point of hiring data-savvy people as you move forward. It's not too hard to assess for this skill set, get them to talk through scenarios to illustrate their analytical thinking, and give tests for numeracy skills. They don't necessarily need to have education in a quantitative subject—someone with a degree in English Literature could have a fine analytical mind.

While it's useful to hire for data-savvy, it's a good idea to look for business-savvy at the same time. Success in analytics depends on starting with the right business question. Green suggests bringing people who have worked in the business into HR—that gives them a big head start in ensuring they focus analytics on relevant business issues.

Ensuring People Analytics Has an Impact

In the stories in this book, there is never any question of HR analytics having an impact on the business because it's driven by the head of HR, who is part of the core executive team. It's not always that easy. Sometimes HR analytics groups do clever work that's either overlooked by the business or not relevant to their immediate needs. If analytics is overlooked or seen as irrelevant, it will be hard to grow it into being a natural part of how HR operates. Green argues that it is important that the person responsible for analytics reports directly to the CHRO—this both signals its importance and ensures analytics is given adequate strategic direction. This reporting level also makes it easier to get access to data and to take action once the analysis is done.

Hopefully, this drive toward a culture of analytics does not appear too daunting. Green agrees that it's important just to get going—focus on the most important issues (since there is always more demand for analytics than supply of time) and use what evidence you have to inform decisions. Don't wait for perfection, just start using data to inform your judgment and add credibility to your recommendations.

Takeaways

- Start analytics early so that making decisions based on data becomes the natural way for HR to operate.
- Don't wait to start sharing people data with colleagues in the C-suite and other leadership roles—it's okay if it has gaps, as long as you can explain why they're there.
- Build the dashboard around questions you want to answer.
- Look for the overall message in a series of metrics. What is the data suggesting?
- Think of HR analytics as answering general management questions such as what they imply for revenue growth or for hitting product deadlines.
- If you don't have stories about how data led to action, then something is wrong.
- Publishing data increases shared accountability.
- Measure what you want to become to keep focused on the future.

Chapter 6
Case Study on a Mosaic of Measures

A simplified look at an executive briefing on organizational health using data.

Guiding the Strategic Conversation on Talent

The HR leader must be one of the business leaders crafting strategy.

I thought it would be helpful to walk through a strategic presentation, about HR, to an executive team. The goal is to get to the point and simply answer the question at hand. It doesn't require highly sophisticated analysis; it's a framework that everyone can easily follow. It provides an example that illustrates the role of data and it shows how you can have an impact with basic data that any HR department should be able to get its hands on.

As you'll see, the presentation is packed full of numbers, and this is why you need someone who can do analytics early on in a company's history, but note that this presentation isn't about "analytics." This presentation is about the strategic issues the top leadership team cares about. That is, to speak intelligently and convincingly about strategic issues.

You'll notice that there is nothing more advanced in the math that underlies this presentation than grade school arithmetic. The advantage of operating at that level is that it's easy for the executive team to digest quickly—we never need to step back and spend fifteen minutes trying to explain some statistical technique—and it is also easy for us to do at this stage of the company's maturation. I'd love to do more sophisticated things like conjoint analysis, but it's amazing how far you can get with just basic counts and percentages.

Another point worth noticing is that we avoid reams of data that would lead the audience to drift into unconsciousness. There is always a story to be told—it's the story that plays the lead, and the numbers validate and illustrate the story. The executive team doesn't really care that there are many, many pages of numbers that got culled out of the analysis; they don't need the whole story about how you narrowed the analysis to just a few select points. The analytics are not the point, so we don't lead with the data and how we got it; we stay focused on the business issue.

DOI 10.1515/9781547400515-006

Starting with the End in Mind

Being clear about the desired outcome before we begin telling the story.

'Broadly speaking, as the HR leader I have to determine and communicate which HR levers (e.g., hiring, training, reward, etc.) have the biggest impact on executing the business strategy. I need to discuss any place where HR factors will undermine the execution of business strategy. From there, we, the executive team, need to either take some actions (such as making an investment in talent acquisition) or be aware of the dynamics such that appropriate actions may be taken (such as correcting imbalances in the organizational structure)."

While it's clear that I have a desired outcome from the presentation, this isn't a sales pitch. Often HR professionals seem to want advice on how they can sell their projects to top management, but that's not the right stance. Here HR is a part of top management, so the desired outcome is the same for HR as for everyone else on the executive team: to succeed in achieving a range of agreed upon business objectives. The pitch is simply to communicate as clearly and convincingly as possible what we know how to achieve those business objectives.

The example that follows illustrates a situation that is very common for growing technology firms. Growing firms have ambitious business goals; to achieve those goals they need to hire a lot of new people, and if they fail to hire those people they won't achieve those goals. The leadership teams need the HR leader to forecast the path forward so there is a predictable future. If decisions need to be made, then they are made early on, not after a crisis hits.

Setting the Stage

Start by getting people on the same page and showing them where we're going.

This portion of the presentation focuses on the talent acquisition challenges in the context of the business strategy. The leadership team has a lot on their minds, so you need to quickly take them through the data on talent acquisition, highlighting the issues, the impact of those issues, and of course, what decisions needed to be considered.

The first slide, Figure 6.1, is designed to get everyone focused and on the same page. CEOs have told me more than once that this is their favorite kind of slide because it is such a simple way to lay out the hiring challenge. In this example, there is a "stretch goal" that the business is shooting for and a more readily achievable goal we call the "commit goal."

XXX - YYY hires remaining this year

	EOY Approved	Q3 Starting HC	Δ in 2018 (EOY - Q3 Starting)	Attrition (Based on H1)	Stretch Goal	Starts + Accepts	Hires Remaining	Commit Goal
					Total Hires (Q3 Onward)			Hires Expected*
Professional	50	40	10	2	12	2	10	10
G&A	100	80	20	5	25	4	21	18
Operations	150	120	30	10	40	4	44	38
Technology	100	80	20	5	25	4	29	15
IT	50	40	10	2	12	2	14	12
Total	450	360	90	24	114	16	118	93

Figure 6.1: Hiring targets

The table in Figure 6.1 has a row for each of the five main departments and shows the amount of hiring required. It's quite simple, but let me walk you through it column-by-column.

If we start with the first row, Professional, we see the End of Year Approved hires is 50, and in the next column that the Third Quarter Starting Headcount (i.e., the current headcount, since we were in the third quarter) was 40. As the figure shows, 50 minus 40 is 10, which is the "delta" between the headcount we have now and the headcount we need by year-end. We tend to add in the hires we'll need due to Attrition for the Total Number of Hires to achieve our Stretch Goal (to fill all approved positions). We then subtract the people about to come on board (Starts + Accepts) to get the final Hires Remaining number. The final column, Commit Goal/Hires Expected, gives the numbers of hires we are confident we can achieve.

The implication of this slide is first that if anyone on the team didn't agree with the numbers, they should speak up. Second, it implies that we had some hiring challenges that we needed to look into more deeply.

A Model of the Constraints on Hiring

Clearly identify the factors the team needs to focus on.

Now that we have everyone on the same page, we want to get them to focus on the three factors that will let us determine whether or not they would be able to achieve the commit goals and stretch goals. These three factors are:

- *Time:* How long it takes leaders to do the hiring in their unit. A leader has about 2,080 hours in a year and only so much of that can be devoted to interviewing candidates. If leaders don't have enough time, then the organization won't achieve its hiring targets and hence won't achieve its business goals.
- *Capacity:* This refers to the capacity the recruiting function has in order to provide quality candidates to be interviewed. Capacity is a function of the number of recruiters and how many positions a recruiter can close in a year.
- *Volume:* The volume of candidates in the pipeline needs to be sufficient for the recruiters to do their work. If there are insufficient candidates in the pipeline, then it won't matter how many recruiters there are.

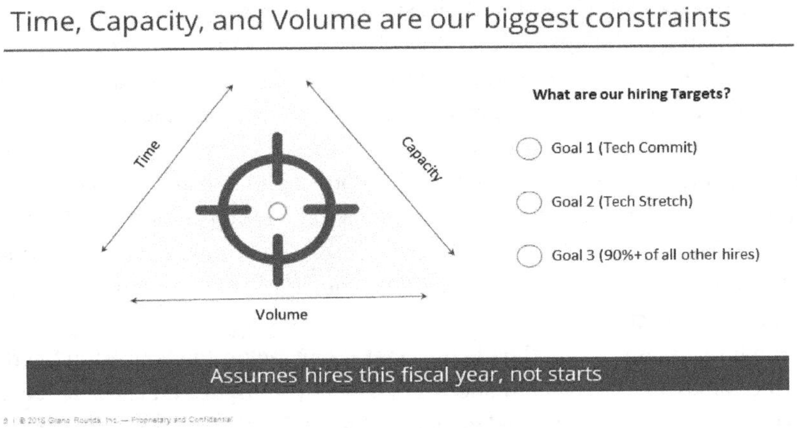

Figure 6.2: The three constraints on hiring

In Figure 6.2, we see the three constraining factors (time, capacity, and volume) around the image of a rifle site aiming at our hiring goal. On the right, I've listed the three goals we want to focus on. The "Tech Commit" goal of how many technology hires we are confident we can make, the "Tech Stretch" goal which would be harder to achieve, and then "Goal 3," which is hitting 90% of the approved hires in all other departments.

The implication of this slide is that these are the only three factors, so if anyone in the leadership team wants to talk about other recruitment factors, they had better say so.

Jumping to the Conclusion

Don't hold leaders in suspense.

It is tempting to slowly build up an argument from the foundations and eventually have it all come together into a compelling conclusion. Leaders hate that approach. Leaders want to know what your conclusion is first and see if you can back it up. The intention with the next slide is to lay out the main conclusion—the one that would grab the team's attention and get them thinking about what actions we might need to take.

Note how HR is collaborating with the leadership team in looking ahead to potential problems and setting the basis for shared ownership for solving them. Sometimes we use terms like "collaboration" and "shared ownership" without being clear about what they really are or how they can be achieved. Neither collaboration nor shared ownership need to be addressed by a special HR initiative—they come from the ongoing way HR interacts with the rest of the leadership team. It seems pretty obvious when I lay it out with some simple slides, but the whole positioning of this presentation is illustrative of how an HR leader sets the right tone with their peers on the leadership team.

Goal 1 is possible and time is our greatest limitation

Goals	Capacity	Volume	Time	Possible Accelerators
Goal 1 (Tech Commit)	✓	✓	✕	• Leaders trained on CTOs approach to hiring
Goal 2 (Tech Stretch)	✕	✕	✕	• Generating higher quality pipeline • High quality referrals from team
Goal 3 (90% of all other hires)	✓	✓	✓	

Figure 6.3: What goals are achievable?

The slide shown in Figure 6.3 uses the traditional coloring scheme of green, yellow, and red to show what is on track, what is marginal, and what is a problem. The rows show each of the three goals we introduced in the previous slides and the columns show the three constraints of capacity, volume, and time. The table makes clear that the stretch goal for hiring technology professionals (Goal 2) is not going to be possible without changes. Even the less ambitious target for technology hiring (Goal 1) has a potential problem with the volume of candidates and definitely a problem with leaders' time.

The final column the slide shows some possible solutions. For example, since the leader most responsible for technology hiring is the CTO, getting other leaders trained in this approach to hiring could take off some of the time pressure. The next two suggestions relate to improving the volume of quality candidates either through the usual pipeline or through referrals.

The implication that HR wants leaders to grasp is that they are going to have to make some business decisions to deal with the predicted problems before they become actual problems. Of course, before any decisions are made, the leadership team will want to see the data that leads to this conclusion.

Drilling Down on Capacity

Provide the data that leaders need to decide on the necessary actions.

Having made some bold conclusions, the intent is then to walk through just a few slides so that the leadership team can be confident that what is suggested is grounded in good data. It will give them a chance to test any assumptions and point out anything that has been overlooked.

The first slide in this part of the presentation looks at the capacity the recruiting team has to fill these jobs for each of the three goals.

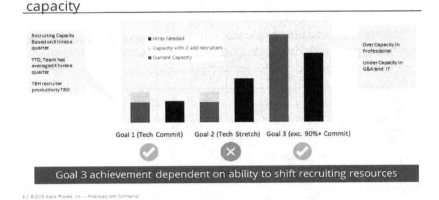

Figure 6.4: An analysis of recruiting capacity

If you compare Figure 6.4 to 6.3 you can see we took the Capacity column (which showed green, red, green from top to bottom) and arranged it horizontally. For each of the three goals there are columns comparing the existing capacity to the goal. In this example, for Goal 1 there is the capacity to match the goal or exceed the goal by adding two new recruiters. The callout box to the left of the columns shows how capacity is calculated. If leaders want more information on any of the elements of the chart, your analytics team should be able to provide that; they would have needed it to create this slide, but there is no need to show all their work.

The second set of columns shows that even with two new recruiting hires, this company wouldn't have the capacity to achieve its Tech Stretch goal. Goal 3 did not appear to be in trouble; although, the callout text on the far right of the slide notes that within this set of open positions we might need to shift recruiting resources from Professional (where there was over-capacity) to G&A and IT, where there was under-capacity.

The implication is that we would need to invest in recruiting capacity (i.e., hire more recruiters) if we wanted to hit Goal 2.

Drilling Down on Volume

How strong is the pipeline of candidates?

The problem with recruiting is that if any one of the three elements (capacity, volume, or time) is lacking, then results will fall short. We've covered the issue of capacity—now the next step is to show the leadership team where the company stands on pipeline volume.

Volume: Optimistic view of the world to achieving hires

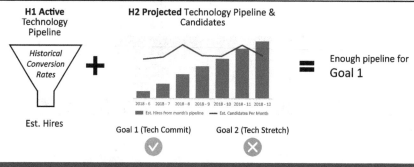

Figure 6.5: A look at the historical volume of candidates

The funnel image on the left in Figure 6.5 captures the fundamental nature of recruiting and highlights how similar it is to sales. The idea is that hopefully a whole lot of potential candidates enter the funnel at the top; as they go through the process, many are screened out or drop out, leaving just a few hires at the end of the process. The conversion rate referenced on the image of the funnel is the percentage of candidates this company has historically been able to convert to hires. Assuming that the company can maintain the conversion rate, they are able to predict the numbers of hires they will be able to make based on how many candidates are at the top of the funnel.

The chart with columns shows how the volume of hires from the funnel has been growing month to month. If we add the "H1 Active funnel" volume to the volume we expect to get from the "H2 Projected pipeline", then there is enough volume to meet Goal 1. (This is explained a bit further in the next Figure.)

At the bottom of the slide, you can see Goal 1 as a checkmark, but in yellow because it's based on a somewhat optimistic projection—even an optimistic projection isn't enough to meet Goal 2.

The implication is that there is a bit of risk with Goal 1 if they don't do anything new, but they'll probably make it. The leadership team will have to consider whether they can live with this risk.

We then move on to provide a bit more insight on the challenges with candidate volume.

Volume: Theoretically, enough pipeline today for non-Tech Roles

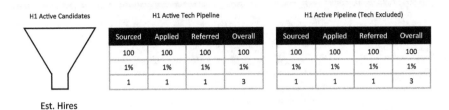

H1 Active Candidates	H1 Active Tech Pipeline				H1 Active Pipeline (Tech Excluded)			
	Sourced	Applied	Referred	Overall	Sourced	Applied	Referred	Overall
	100	100	100	100	100	100	100	100
	1%	1%	1%	1%	1%	1%	1%	1%
	1	1	1	3	1	1	1	3
Est. Hires								

Niche roles may be more challenging to fill than conversion suggest

Figure 6.6: Is the candidate volume sufficient?

The second slide on candidate volume, Figure 6.6, provides illustrative numbers only. It shows three main sources of hire that feed the H1 active pipeline: candidates sourced by recruiting agencies; candidates who have applied to advertisements, and candidates who were referred. The rows show the raw number, the conversion rate, and hence the total number of hires. In this figure, we used 100 for the raw number in each case to simplify the example. You would enter in your raw data for each category, and your conversion rate to get your total expected number of hires.

Drilling Down on Time

How much time does it take to hire a new employee?

You don't want to drown the leadership team in data, but you do need to take them through the last big constraint on hiring: leadership time.

Time: It takes about X weeks to close a tech req

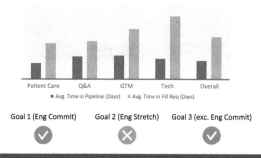

Figure 6.7: The time constraint on technology hires

In Figure 6.7 we look, for each department, at how long a candidate is in the pipeline and how long it takes to fill a job opening once we have a requisition. The reason the numbers are different is that when there are strong candidates who are likely to be hired, most companies are pretty good at accelerating the process. However, the more important column is the second one: the average time to fill, since that tells us how many jobs the company can expect to fill in the available time.

There is one more point that I've used in this sort of presentation that I think is worth sharing. It turns out the time it takes different teams to make a hire can be dramatically different.

Figure 6.8: Time spent on hiring in different departments

In Figure 6.8 the average time the hiring team spends per hire is shown for each area. The implication is that some teams may be spending too much time and other teams may be spending too little.

What You Can Learn from This Presentation

In some ways this is just a basic presentation of facts, but you can imagine that a lot of work goes into pulling this data together; of course, the few numbers shown here are the tip of the iceberg and are all supported by many more calculations that you would make available in an appendix.

As simple as this presentation is, it does capture some of the characteristics of an analytics-savvy HR function. We are focused on a business issue that puts us in collaboration and shared ownership with the leadership team. We have a clear idea of the decisions that need to be grappled with, and we can back that up with data. We keep it as simple as we can, while providing enough data so that the leadership team both understands the situation and has confidence that HR has based this limited set of data on a deeper analysis.

Takeaways

- Analytics doesn't need to be sophisticated to be useful
- Tell a story that starts with the business issue
- Keep it short and simple; don't drown your audience in data

Chapter 7
How We Handled HR Technology and Processes

If the goal of the HR function is to create a strategic advantage, then it can't let itself get bogged down in transactions; technology is the answer.

Why HR Technology Is a High Priority

Think through when and how much to invest in HR technology.

Historically, HR has done a lot on administrative paperwork. If you are building a new company, then it's typical to follow that same trajectory, starting with loose manual processes and then gradually formalizing and automating them. From the viewpoint of a CMO of People, whose mission is to drive business impact, the notion of HR doing manual processes is distasteful. We just don't want to be a department staffed with people who push paper.

In Section 5.1, we argued that you should hire an analytics team before some traditional HR roles. You'll see much the same thinking when it comes to technology. The CMO of People model leans toward an early investment in technology as part of a sustainable foundation because it's easy to get trapped in manual work and processes that don't scale. This trap of manual work will seriously handcuff attempts to have an impact on the business.

Leaning toward early investments in technology shouldn't be confused with wanting to have all the latest gizmos. I never sought technology that people felt was really cool; I just wanted the basics that would free up my team to do their real work. I had a clear vision of what I wanted the HR organization to be, and then pushed back against tendencies that would take us in the wrong direction—tendencies like putting up with a lot of manual administrative work.

As always, it's a question of whether a piece of technology is a good investment. However, our executive team didn't look at return on investment in narrow terms, such as how much headcount some HR technology might save. We looked at how HR technology, or the lack of HR technology, would affect the overall growth trajectory of the business. If recruitment or onboarding technology would help us grow an effective sales force faster, that is where the strategic payoff would be found. If you are a rapidly growing company, you'll want to lean toward early investment in technology because it will get you where you need to be faster.

DOI 10.1515/9781547400515-007

What Happens When Technology Is Prioritized

Properly done, technology implementation creates a simple, efficient process. Improperly used, it acts as a constraint that prevents HR from straying into ad hoc, customized, or inefficient solutions. If HR people start doing administrative work, then that's what they are likely to continue doing. If they start with a clear, straightforward system such that administration is minimized, then they'll focus on other things.

It's also true that if you create a process and then try to automate it, chances are that you'll find your process doesn't fit very well with how the vendor's software works. This creates a whole load of extra work as you decide where you can redesign the process and where you need to pay for expensive software customization. That's another reason to lean toward an early investment in technology.

Implications for Choosing Technology

If one of the purposes of technology is to avoid the trap of manual processes, then the main things you want out of a technology, beyond the basic fit with your requirements, are ease of use and integration.

Ease of use for the customer is part of the design and adoption consideration. It is a priority because people don't have time to master complex HR software; you should be willing to sacrifice features for ease of use. Again, it comes down to having a clear vision of how the HR function is driving value via an experience that improves productivity and performance. We don't get overly enamored with HR software because our focus is on the business, not on HR.

Integration is a priority because lack of integration can be a huge time-waster for HR—in fact, it can obliterate any time-savings that the technology would otherwise deliver. You should be willing to pay more if that's what it takes to get integrated software, or else invest the time to ensure that the points of integration are easily handled. Integration is more complicated than you might imagine because there are many different levels. You can't simply rely on a vendor's claim that their software will easily integrate with your other systems. You need to work with an internal or external expert who can advise you just what is involved in integrating two particular systems, what the limitations of the integration are, and how easy it will be to maintain that integration as the different systems are upgraded.

Yet in the End It's Not About Technology, It's About Outcomes

Important as it is, HR technology on its own won't achieve much—you need effective program management and a clear view of the outcomes. In fact, in one case, the performance management software we had was undeniably lousy. We got around this by getting everyone focused on the end results we needed to achieve. The focus was on the outcome, not the tool, and we could admit the tool was poor and then figure out how to best work around it to get the outcomes we all agreed mattered to the business.

To get the benefits of technology, people need how to use it, why to use it, and most of all the business outcomes HR is aiming to achieve. This is easy to say but hard to do because we get sucked so deeply into the details of the technology that it's hard to look up at the bigger purpose.

Design Perspective

The normal perspective on HR tech focuses on the importance of efficiency, having a single source of truth, and compliance. Those all are important, and to go deeper, a design perspective urges us to lean back and determine the purpose of the technology.

So a design perspective would lead us to ask, "What is the problem the tech is meant to solve?" and "Is it actually solving it?" This perspective would lead to prioritizing measures on how often it is being used (i.e., adoption rate). If it's online training, then we'd not just want to know that it is available, but also whether it is being used and making employees more productive. Even though you can't get precise answers to those questions, any indicators are helpful.

Technology, like analytics, tends to draw us into the weeds; we need to make an effort to keep perspective and stay focused on the basic processes that will have an impact on the business. Let's consider a technology I know well: DocuSign. It is a nice technology for cutting back on admin work, but the bigger perspective is that it helps people to sign up faster and hence gets them off the job market and into your firm.

What Can You Do Today?

Consider shifting investment out of some existing HR projects and into technology. Consider what would happen if you accelerated your HR technology roadmap. Could you start eliminating large swaths of low-value transactional work?

How Technology Fits with HR Analytics

We used technology to support HR analytics.

In Chapter 5, I stressed the primacy of HR analytics. In Section 7.1, I argued that HR technology should also be a priority, superseding investment in more traditional HR work. You might expect that this mindset would lead to a highly sophisticated HR analytics technology infrastructure. That isn't necessarily the case.

The Link Between Technology and Analytics

Core HR technology does two separate things: it enables efficient transactions and it captures data to enable analytics. In implementing technology, one has to ensure that the right data is being captured (and captured accurately).

The right data points toward answers about:
- What is happening?
- Is it important enough to worry about?
- Why is it happening?
- What can I do about it?

For example, it's typical for a modern applicant tracking system to provide some data on the candidate funnel so that you can see when candidates are dropping out. However, knowing what has happened isn't enough—you need to know why, and for that you'd need to collect feedback on the candidate experience. Once you know why candidates are dropping out, you are in a position to consider what to do about it.

I had this experience in one organization where we were getting too many candidates dropping out. Each member of the recruiting team had different opinions for the cause of the dropouts. I couldn't prioritize which opinion to act on in the absence of data. The systems were just managing workflow, not gathering the data I needed for decision-making. Until we fixed the systems to gather candidate experience data, we were just guessing about what changes would help.

In addition to core HR technology that provides data, there are now many tools aimed specifically to help with HR analytics. We didn't lean heavily on technology to provide advanced analytics. The main point of analytics is to go from a world of no numbers to one with some numbers. We needed to answer questions like, "How long does it take a new sales rep to develop to the point they can hit their quota?" and "How many software engineers will we have by the end of the quarter given our talent pipeline?" Actually, we could be more accurate in framing those questions. We needed to know, "*Roughly* how long..." and "*Approximately* how many..." and we would get answers that were close enough for managers to make decisions, not highly precise predictive models. To get rough but adequate answers to these questions, we needed to get basic data from our systems, and then analyze it in Excel—that was about it.

Image courtesy of Visier Inc.

Figure 7.1: Metrics used to track the candidate funnel

The simple display of the candidate funnel in Figure 7.1 shows how useful technology can be in moving to a world where data is our friend. The image simply lists each of the steps of the hiring process, starting with Applied, then Screened, then Qualified, right through to Hire Yet to Start. The horizontal bars show the number of candidates at each step. If there is a problem in the process, such as too few of those passing the Screening stage and making it through the Qualifying stage, or (toward the end of the process) too few Offers Accepted, then it shows up clearly on the screen.

The great thing about having this kind of technology is that the data doesn't stop with what you see on the screen—you can dig deeper to investigate any problems or anomalies.

Powerful Questions, Before Powerful Tools

The way to get good analytics, without a significant investment in analytics technology, is to be very clear about the questions the business needs answered. We wanted to know what social causes mattered most to employees because that was important to the employment brand. Given that kind of clear question, our analytics team could dig into the data on what matching donations had been requested by employees and pull together an answer on what social issues mattered most. We relied on good questions and a creative analytics team to give us the answers we needed.

Similarly, we did not create a lot of standard HR reports. The focus was always on being able to tell a story grounded in data. The starting point was the business issue we were grappling with and a solution that made sense given the data we had. We didn't feel a need to create reports just because that's what everyone else did.

Most of the mathematics needed for our analyses was pretty basic. In fact, at that point we did most of the analysis in Excel. When you want to do advanced analytics, then you'll need an advanced tool like Visier; if you just want to make a business decision, then running the numbers through a spreadsheet is often enough.

Low Tech, Big Impact

As we discussed in Chapter 2, a useful analytics project that is particularly relevant to the CMO of People mindset involves developing a "persona" of a successful employee. The concept comes from Marketing, where you develop an idealized portrait of one or more typical customers. We created employee personas that illustrated what makes them successful: how they behaved, what made them stay, and what enabled them to move up in the organization.

What technology did we need to support this important piece of analysis? Nothing much. We gathered basic data on successful employees and used it to inform a discussion of the persona. Even though it was low tech, it had a big impact.

The takeaway is that you want technology to capture data that will be helpful in analytics, but you don't necessarily need a big investment in data warehouses or machine learning.

What Can You Do Today?

Shift away from the thinking that technology will be the answer to your analytics woes. Consider the capability that exists in HR to ask the right questions, and the capability of the analytics team to provide creative answers in a world where data might be limited or scattered.

Examples of How We Built an HR Technology Infrastructure

Here are two examples of an HR technology infrastructure.

Technology changes so quickly that any detailed description can quickly seem dated. Nonetheless, we think that it can be helpful to move from general principles to specifics.

At Shutterfly, the flow of talent acquisition data started with an employer page on LinkedIn, which fed candidates to our applicant tracking system (Jobvite), which, after someone was hired, fed the data into our core HRIS (Workday). From there, the data went into our compensation analysis software (CompExcel) and the results of the analysis were sent back to Workday.

The takeaway is that, in practice, there were quite a few pieces—more than we'd ideally like—but the system worked well since the pieces were integrated to the point that we could easily share data between them.

From a pragmatic point of view, the system allowed us to do our work quickly with minimal administrative burden. From an employment brand perspective, we communicated that we were a technology-friendly organization. We also emphasized mobile access, which seems self-evident now but was less obvious then; that decision flowed from a focus on how the employee experienced the software, not what was convenient for HR.

What we didn't do was just as relevant as what we did. There was no "joke of the day" on the Jive site because that had no relevance to the brand. Similarly, even though Jive recommended that we gamify the communication site, we didn't go that route. We avoided those distractions by being clear about the business purpose of the communication hub: productivity. We wanted employees to get into the software, get what they needed to get done, and then get out. We didn't want people hanging around earning badges. This sounds obvious when I say it this way—however, it should also be easy to see the appeal of a "joke of the day." As CMO of People you need to spend far more time than you'd imagine communicating your vision and jumping on examples like this one to drive home the difference between how you conceptualize HR and how it may be practiced elsewhere.

But It's Not Always That Clean

The Shutterfly example is a nice, clean case of what a mid-sized company can do. At DocuSign, the HR technology grew up focused on point solutions (applications supplying one data point) and we ended up with an enormous set of applications sitting on a single sign-on page. The long-term plan was to consolidate the applications, which isn't that easy to do. It was a lesson on why you need an HR technology roadmap to guide the implementation of HR—without that roadmap, it's natural to end up with an awkward system that is difficult to correct.

The lack of user friendliness in our HR technology showed up in the engagement survey. One question asked, "How easy is it to work here?" and the score was relatively low in part because of the difficulty of using the HR systems.

While the HR systems were not integrated as cleanly as we would have liked, we were successful in integrating data between HR and non-HR systems. This integration allowed our analytics team to do business-focused people analytics. For example, to better understand how salespeople were performing, our analysts needed access to the sales territory system. To understand costs related to the employee experience, such as food and leasing costs, we needed access to the general ledger.

Getting access to non-HR systems can be a political and technical challenge. Sales is usually open to sharing access to its data with anyone who wants to help. Finance, which plays more of a "guardian" role in the organization, can be protective of access to the general ledger. They want to know exactly how the information will be used, but in the end, as we built trust it became easier to get the data we needed.

What Can You Do Today?

It's likely that you'll end up with multiple HR systems. Ensure that there's adequate integration at each handoff so that your HR team isn't wasting time on unnecessary administrative work.

Takeaways

- Investing in technology early prevents HR from falling into the trap of building manual administrative processes that eat up all of HR's time.
- One of the biggest time-wasters is the lack of integration between different pieces of HR software.

- The secret ingredients of successful analytics are good questions and a creative analytics team, not expensive technology.
- If you are growing rapidly, then you need to bite the bullet and make a hefty investment in HR technology that will scale with your organization.

Chapter 8
Unconventional HR Leaders and the Role of the CEO

A CMO of People strategy calls for an unconventional HR leader.

Why Your Company Might Want an Unconventional CHRO

Is there (or should there be) an appetite for unconventional HR in your business?

Let's stop to consider how the CMO of People approach looks from the viewpoint of the CEO and the Board. The CMO of People model is unconventional, which raises the question of whether your organization should be looking for an unconventional CHRO. Historically, CHROs lived in a world of administration, compliance, and providing services to the business. That is all necessary work, but it won't transform a company. Rick Jensen, SVP, Chief Talent Officer at Intuit, observes that the best HR programs originate as small experiments in the business that scale over time—rather than big programs that come out of HR fully formed.

If you want HR programs that grow out of the business, in a test and learn approach, then it may help to have someone who doesn't fit the mold of the traditional HR leader.

Your current CHRO might be less conventional in their thinking than you presume. There are a lot of talented HR leaders who are more constrained by their company's expectations than by their own lack of vision. If the CEO changes the mandate of the HR function, HR might rise to the occasion.

Alternatively, you might want to bring in a less conventional CHRO from outside the company. An ideal candidate would have a mix of line management and HR experience. Unfortunately, the demand for business savvy HR leaders outstrips the supply, which means that you should consider going outside of the HR talent pipeline for a CHRO. Bringing in a business leader without an HR background to lead HR has significant risks, but in some cases, it's your best bet.

DOI 10.1515/9781547400515-008

Do CEOs Know What They Want?

It can be an interesting exercise to ask a CEO to describe how they personally do people management (i.e. picking, motivating, and rewarding their executive team) and then comparing that to the goals they set for their HR leader. What they want is often couched in terms of getting a competitive advantage from talent, and what they ask for is typically oversight of the core HR operations. Once CEOs are aware of this discrepancy, they are more open to an HR leader who can help them architect a systemic, sustainable solution in a conventional or unconventional way—that's where the potential of a true strategic partnership lives.

What Can You Do Today?

Consider if the expectations of leadership are getting in the way of HR being more proactive and business focused. Is there a part of the business that gets more out of HR because it sets better expectations? Can the enterprise as a whole adopt the mindset of the business unit that has the best relationship with HR?

How to Convince a Non-HR Professional to Lead HR

CEOs are often attracted to the idea of bringing in a non-HR leader to run HR—is this wise?

If HR isn't sufficiently business savvy, why not bring in a business leader from another function to be CHRO? This might sound good to a CEO, but convincing a successful business leader to move into HR isn't easy.

Phil Johnston, an executive search leader at Spencer Stuart, said, "When a CEO asks a business leader to run HR, the most frequent response is, 'What did I do wrong?' It's not seen as a desirable role; it's seen as punishment. Of course, they haven't had a chance to think it through—it's just the first reaction."

I interviewed HR leaders from non-traditional backgrounds about how it came to pass that they landed in HR. Their initial reactions to being offered the job were similar—they said, "I thought it was a joke," "I flat out refused," and "I was totally surprised."

The leaders I interviewed eventually relented and took on the CHRO role because the CEO was able to sell the upside and wouldn't take no for an answer. When Lucia Luce Quinn was being recruited out of a business development role to lead HR at Boston Scientific, she repeatedly said no. Quinn said, "What finally sold me on the CHRO role was that three board members asked me to breakfast and they explained why they needed a non-HR person in the role, and it had everything to do with getting ready for CEO succession with a potential acquisition. When it was clear why they absolutely needed me for the role, I was willing to take it on."

If your organization is considering sourcing a CHRO from a non-HR background, then be prepared to make a compelling case about the strategic importance of the role, and how it is the best possible move for their career.

The idea that it's a good career move isn't just a sales pitch. A December, 2014 HBR article, "Why Chief Human Resource Officers Make Great CEOs," cited research by Dave Ulrich, professor of business at the Ross School of Business, University of Michigan, and Korn Ferry's Ellie Filler, showing the competencies of a CEO matched the competencies of a CHRO better than any other function. In light of this research, the CHRO role might be more than a great job; it could be the natural stepping stone to the CEO's office in the future.

What It's Like to Be CHRO for Someone with a Non-Traditional Background

Quinn sums up the experience of a business leader who had shifted into HR: "I don't love telling people I'm in HR, but I love leading HR. As CHRO, I use every skill I ever learned." We heard similar stories from other leaders; they were surprised to find the enormous scope, freedom, and power that lie within the CHRO role. In many ways, HR is the least siloed department in an organization. Every part of the organization has leadership and talent challenges. Every problem and every opportunity have a people-dimension. There is no issue in any part of the company, at any level, where HR cannot play a crucial role.

Imagine that the problem is excess inventory. While that might not sound like a traditional HR problem, for a non-traditional HR leader it falls clearly in their domain. They will ask, "Are the incentives leading people to build up unnecessary inventory? Have we designed the inventory management job correctly? Do we have the right people in the role? Is our training adequate? Do we have communication problems that are leading to the excess inventory?" Through the eyes of the right business leader, HR is the most strategic function in the organization.

Of course, the typical HR business partner isn't trained to ask questions such as these, nor are they expected to ask them. That's a barrier for a non-traditional CHRO and it's also their opportunity to make a difference by elevating the business-savvy of all the roles within HR.

What Type of Experience Makes for a Good Non-Traditional CHRO?

From the viewpoint of the CMO of People model, the most natural place to look for a non-traditional CHRO is Marketing. Brad Brooks, CEO at OneLogin former CMO at DocuSign, says, "I absolutely would consider bringing a former CMO to become CHRO because there is so much alignment in the demeanor and skill set. It works both ways—I'd consider taking a high-level HR leader and put them in charge of Marketing. More generally, it makes sense for people to do some rotation between Marketing and HR at some point in their career."

However, the successful non-traditional CHROs I spoke to came from a wide variety of backgrounds. Brooks nailed it when he said, "The most important thing to appreciate is the strategic importance of the HR function; it's taking on a different level of strategic relevance and importance." Someone who understands this is at the right starting point to transform HR.

I liked a comment that Quinn made about appreciating the strategic importance of HR. She said that she didn't talk about the management of the HR function—she talked about business issues. Often, I hear HR people say things like, "We have to get better assessment tools for HR because our business strategy depends on talent." That's not wrong, but it still focuses more on management of the HR function and less on business issues. If you're looking for an unconventional HR leader, look for someone who talks about the business, not about HR.

Note: The quotes from Johnston and Quinn come from our May 2017 HBR online article with John Boudreau, "Why More Executives Should Consider Becoming a CHRO."

What Can You Do Today?

Send a note around your network to see if anyone worked with an HR leader who didn't come from HR. Arrange for a chat so that they can tell you how it worked out.

Relevant Skills a CMO Brings to HR

HR can be an exciting role for someone coming from a marketing background because many of the skills are transferable:
- A customer-focused mindset (easily translates to an employee-focused mindset)
- Analytics savvy (a skill now standard in Marketing but highly sought after in HR)
- Ability to construct a compelling story (getting managers and employees to embrace change requires effective storytelling)
- Experience with a test-and-learn approach (marketing has long done test marketing, but with the advent of digital marketing their expertise with a test-and-learn approach has grown enormously)

Is the CMO of People Role Right for You?

The CMO of People role has a lot of appeal. Is it right for you?

I talked about hiring a non-traditional CHRO from the viewpoint of a CEO. What about for you personally? Is the role of transforming HR as a CMO of People, or some other unconventional model, right for you?

One way to think about it is to understand that success is defined in this formula:

$$Analytics \times Iteration \times Curiosity = Influence + Confidence$$

Does this sound like you? Recipes for HR success are often treated as an additive set of features; our experience suggests the success function is multiplicative. HR leaders achieve influence and confidence through the combination of the factors above, and they must balance and reinforce each other.

One of my favorite role models for "analytics, iteration, and curiosity" is Paul Baldassari, CHRO of Flex, a global manufacturer of technology. He's always asking, "What can we do differently? What can we test out and learn from? What does the data show?"

As a role model for "influence and confidence," you can't do better than Jacqueline Reses, Chief Human Resources Officer at Square, a mobile payment company based in San Francisco. She said, "HR must trust more in their power and influence and enjoy the enormous freedom the role provides. My biggest issue was to get my HR colleagues to understand the power of their voice and influence."

Do the Views of Baldassari and Reses Resonate with You?

Another way of looking at the CMO of People role is to review characteristics that appeared in our interviews with non-traditional HR leaders. Look through the list below to see how the list matches your interests and abilities.

– *General management (rather than a functional) perspective.* The head of HR is usually seen as a functional head, which implies that their contribution comes from managing their function well. A general management perspective looks at the business as a whole. An unconventional HR leader is pulling the HR levers while seeing issues the same way a business unit head would. That is, that the company's goals are HR leaders' goals.

- *Collaboration.* HR can only transform a business if it's working very closely with other members of the C-suite. This can be hard work—it can feel like it's slowing things down. However, if collaboration comes naturally, then you have one of the core competencies for an unconventional HR leader.
- *Systems thinking.* Transformation depends on getting a host of elements aligned; that requires systems thinking—the ability to see how different parts of the system interconnect. For example, you could hire more experienced people and spend less on training but more on compensation, or hire less experienced people and pay less but spend more on training—each element affects the other.
- *Data-driven.* Unconventional moves won't get leadership support unless the head of HR proves that their decisions are grounded in data.
- *Risk orientation and curiosity.* One peculiar thing in our interviews with HR leaders who had non-HR backgrounds was their gleeful response to risk. When faced with a big challenge, they became extremely energized. This came packaged with endless curiosity. Unconventional leaders are always fascinated by what would happen if they did things differently (and are willing to try it to see).
- *Adaptability and dealing with ambiguity.* Closely related to the idea of loving risk is a high tolerance for ambiguity. Much of traditional HR is about driving out ambiguity with clear rules and well-defined processes. If you thrive on clarity, then you might not be comfortable with the CMO of People approach.

What Can You Do Today?

Ask a friend how they see you in terms of the six characteristics we've seen in unconventional HR leaders. How do their observations compare to your views of your strengths?

How to Grow HR Leaders Who Understand Business

The HR talent pipeline isn't growing enough business savvy HR leaders.

The long-term goal for an organization is to grow HR leaders internally with, as a matter of course, the business focus and strategic knowledge required for the CMO of People approach. I keep talking about unconventional CHROs, but in an ideal world, these business-savvy HR professionals would be the norm, not the exception.

There are three main tactics for growing HR leaders who understand the business: who you hire, their development experiences, and the expectations set for them.

Hiring HR Professionals Who Can Grow into Business-Savvy Leaders

David Almeda, Chief People Officer of Kronos, has played a big role as a member of the leadership team driving Kronos' growth. It is a $1.3 billion company that has delivered 9% compound annual growth over the last five years, while also successfully transforming from an on-premise to a cloud technology provider. It regularly lands on many "best places to work" lists and gets enviable ratings on Glassdoor (CEO Aron Ain is one of the highest rated CEOs on Glassdoor). Almeda has made a special effort to make the HR functions business focused and data savvy. A big part of this effort is hiring the right people. Almeda says that Kronos doesn't need special assessment tools to determine which candidates have this business focus—if you are looking for it, then it stands out. Once you move the HR function in this direction, then eventually a business-savvy culture takes hold and it becomes the normal way for HR to operate.

When Almeda relates a great example of how Kronos uses data and evidence to make better HR decisions—for example, using the marketing tool of conjoint analysis to find which benefits matter most to employees—he often caps the story with, "It doesn't feel like we're doing anything exceptional." That's the right attitude to instill in young HR professionals: a business / data focus isn't special—it's just the normal way that HR ought to work.

Formative Developmental Experiences

There is nothing better for developing an understanding of the business than actually working in the business. Certainly, aiming to rotate people in and out of HR is a good idea. However, many organizations report that this kind of rotation is difficult to do. You might have to accept a compromise of getting HR people to simply spend as much time with the business as possible, and to work on multi-disciplinary teams, so that they get a feel for what it's like.

One enlightening observation is how often I hear HR people saying, "I'm not really an HR person—I started in sales," or "I'm not really an HR person—I'm an engineer." This seems fair enough, but when you dig into their history, you'll find that they spent the last ten or twenty years in HR and you have to go back to the earliest days of their career to find them working in another function. Luckily, that might not matter. It seems the formative experiences of working in the business can shape your perspective throughout a career.

Almeda is an interesting example because he is an HR leader who has frequently been entrusted with operational responsibilities beyond HR. However, Almeda points out that he's spent almost his entire career in HR roles, so where does that business savvy originate? He can only point back to his earliest job as an eighteen-year-old running a section of a grocery store. Formative experiences can go a long way. It might not be necessary for HR professionals to have a lot of experience outside of HR—just a few significant experiences that have shaped their perspective.

The Right Expectations

Lucia Quinn (see section "How to Convince a Non-HR Professional to Lead HR" earlier in this chapter) said that one of the biggest challenges for HR teams that worked for her was that they didn't have managers who ensured that they understood the business first. There was never an expectation that they should be able to *anticipate* the potential issues.

Rick Jensen noted that to be a great talent acquisition professional, it takes more than being a great recruiter. You have to understand the business short and long, be forward thinking and understand how these roles integrate with the business and how it's scaling. Today, it takes massive business acumen, an understanding of the strategy and where the business is going. HR managers are not the only ones who fail to set the right expectations for young HR professionals; business leaders often fall short as well. Business leaders might never have worked with an unconventional HR department so they don't know what to ask for.

If HR professionals are underperforming, it is natural to think that you need to hire different people, train them differently, or that they need better developmental experiences. Perhaps all they need is someone to set the right expectations and then empower them to deliver by getting the low value transactional work off their plates.

What Can You Do Today?

Identify some sharp people in your company who are outside of HR who you would like to join the function. Think about how you will begin to do the wooing and politicking that will bring them into the HR department.

How It Can All Go Wrong

Make no mistake: bringing in a business leader to run HR is risky.

There's a story about award-winning novelist Margaret Atwood attending a fancy dinner party. She happened to be sitting beside a surgeon who turned to her and said, "It's a real pleasure to meet you. You know, after I retire, I'm thinking of becoming a novelist." Atwood smiled sweetly and replied, "What an amazing coincidence. When I retire, I'm thinking of becoming a surgeon."

HR professionals often have a similar reaction when someone proposes bringing in a business leader to run HR. They react to the implication that HR professionals are not business leaders. More seriously, they roll their eyes at the notion that their profession is so simple that someone with no experience in it could do a great job.

The biggest risk that a CEO faces in bringing in someone without HR experience to lead HR is that both the CEO and business leader might be seriously underestimating the knowledge required to successfully run HR.

The Need to Respect the HR Profession

The worst offenders are those who scarcely see HR as a discipline at all. A financial professional might feel that all they need to do is bring financial discipline to the HR department. This is the road to disaster. If a new CHRO from outside HR tries to run the department based solely on their old skill set, they will degrade the company's talent capabilities.

The lesser offenders are those who care about HR without truly appreciating its subtleties. Mike Haffenden, who runs the Corporate Research Forum think tank in the UK, says that the challenge with HR is that there are many initiatives that sound great, but don't deliver value. Humans are notably complex and at times ornery. It takes years of experience to differentiate between programs that look good and those that have a business impact.

The solution is to respect the function and rely on a strong team of experienced HR professionals. Lucia Luce Quinn, an unconventional CHRO who grew up outside the function, tells a story about a time the HR team was feeling depressed about an initiative. She asked why and they said it was because they knew it wouldn't work; they'd done it in previous years and it hadn't delivered business impact. She then asked the obvious question, "If it's not going to work, then why are you doing it?" The answer was that leaders had asked for it and they were just being good HR pros who did what they were told. Quinn, of course, told them to push back and asked them to design an initiative that would work. They did this with great success.

The lesson I want to pull from this story is that Quinn was relying on the HR team's deep professional expertise to come up with an effective alternative. Her role was to help HR re-envision itself as what Dave Ulrich calls "credible activists" and not assume that leaders are always right when they ask for something.

Quinn is quite explicit about how much she relies on having a strong, experienced HR team: "If you want a compensation program or a diversity program, I'm not the specialist. I have opinions, but I look to my team for that specialist expertise."

Rick Jensen, mentioned earlier in this chapter, says, "I work around some phenomenal HR professionals who have been in the business for twenty-five years—and they have a really strong business acumen as well an HR know-how." If a non-traditional HR leader doesn't have deep respect for the profession and doesn't rely on a strong experienced team, they will have real trouble delivering the business results and struggle in the role. Even at the best of times, the transition to HR can be tough. Executive search professionals warn that moves between companies are often difficult, and moves between functional areas are even more difficult. Bringing in a business leader from a different company to run HR combines these two risks to the point that many search professionals advise against it.

The CXO Delusion

One big mistake is to think that the safest way to elevate HR and make it more business focused is to take an existing senior executive and put them in charge of HR—*while retaining their existing functional responsibilities*. This is usually nothing more than knocking HR down a reporting level—the opposite of the goal of elevating the function.

In the CMO of People model, the HR leader is a CXO who handles Real Estate and Workplace Services and CSR, as well as traditional HR. This shouldn't be confused with a combined CFO/CHRO role that is, in practice, nothing more than a VP HR reporting to the CFO.

What Can You Do Today?

Assess the capability of the existing HR staff. Do they have the inherent capability to support a CHRO who isn't an HR expert?

A Method for Mitigating Risk

The CMO of People strategy has a lot of risks. How do you mitigate them?

Many leaders who seek to dramatically transform HR have a strange love for big challenges and leaping into the unknown. This does not mean that they take foolish chances; one reason these leaders have a high appetite for risk is that they've learned how to mitigate risk. CEOs can support change more effectively if they also support tactics for reducing risk.

A very important tactic for mitigating risk is the "test-and-learn" approach. This is almost the opposite of what you might expect from a confident leader hoping to transform a function. If you were making a movie about Chief HR Officers (a genre that Hollywood has, to date, overlooked), then you would expect the transformational leader to be a "damn the torpedoes," "turn everything upside down at once" kind of person. A dramatic approach is good for movies, but in real life, when moving into unknown terrain, test and learn is the way to go.

Test and learn is common in product development where the starting point is the *minimum viable product*. HR programs can be treated the same way: they start in the smallest, simplest way possible—knowing that we're testing, not producing a final product—and gradually improve through multiple iterations.

An example of a successful test-and-learn project
Iterative HR at Flex

Flex is a global organization with 200,000 people in 30 countries. It can take an engineer's idea for a new product and provide the full range of services needed to go from Sketch-to-Scale™ production all the way to making millions of units—and they do it quickly, providing a competitive advantage in an age when cycle times are shorter than ever.

Just as the organization provides rapid, iterative product development for its customers, so too does Human Resources (HR) take a rapid, iterative "test-and-learn" approach on how it delivers its products and services to managers and employees.

A good example is how Flex approaches HR dashboards. It would be natural for HR to go about the process of creating dashboards by consulting users, having internal meetings on what the dashboard should contain, working with designers on the "look" of the dashboard, getting IT staff to build the dashboard, and finally doing a roll-out of communication and training.

This traditional approach is called the waterfall method because you can think of it as a series of cascading waterfalls, where one project is carefully completed before moving on to the next phase.

Paul Baldassari, CHRO at Flex, took a different path. His approach was to quickly get something in the hands of managers, see how they liked it, and then evolve from there. The first project his team focused on was to take the old reports, typically distributed by email, and build a live dashboard that was similar to that the traditional reports. The team got feedback on that prototype from users around the world; they found people on the frontlines also wanted more granular data. In other words, rather than a report which starts with an overview and then you drill down, they wanted the specifics of what was happening in their own area. HR improved the dashboards and got more feedback suggesting people really valued information they'd need to act on. Thanks to that learning, HR added more action-oriented alerts.

The result of the iterative approach was a dashboard that got high usage and high satisfaction. It's unlikely they'd have achieved that without the fast turnaround of prototype-feedback-next prototype-more feedback approach. Baldassari says "We go fast, we make mistakes, and we learn from those mistakes."

An even more interesting example is how they developed workforce planning tools. Flex produces over 10,000 unique new products a year with its customers—everything from cell phones to medical devices. The cycle time for new products is crucial. For example, the cycle time for cell phones was once eighteen months, now it's only five months. The key to creating new products quickly is having the right quality and quantity of talent—hence the need for workforce planning.

As with the dashboard, the implementation team dove in, quickly putting together a tool that, in a complex way, captured all the relevant data. They heard from users that it was challenging to go from the data to relevant insights, so they kept iterating to better tools. The tools evolved in two directions—reactive and proactive.

The reactive use of workforce planning occurs when Flex is quoting a project for a customer. Coming up with an accurate quote is challenging because they are always dealing with new products and innovations. However, because they've done many projects over the years they can look back at the data and estimate how many shop floor people they'll need (e.g. the efficiency of a worker putting screws in a phone) and how many people they'll need in support functions such as engineering or program management, taking into account the expected frequency of change orders. Baldassari said, "We have five hundred different job functions in the company, so you can imagine the complexity, but the advantage of collecting a lot of data over time is having the capability to do good analytics."

The proactive use of workforce planning is the most surprising part of the story. The worst thing that can happen in their industry is to commit to customers to deliver at a certain date only to find you are short a few people in quality control or in engineering and you cannot deliver the service you promised. If this happens, the customer is not happy, and profits can be impacted because huge operational costs are incurred catching up.

When it's clear the challenge is talent and they have the workforce planning tool, HR can be involved in the conversation with the customer and help the business teams give an accurate assessment of when they'll be able to deliver. Customers really appreciate the accuracy, even if it's a later date than was first planned, because it's a commitment they can trust.

Better conversations with customers about what they could deliver was not a part of the original design of workforce planning. Flex wasn't just iterating on features of this business tool, they were iterating on the use case of the tool, with the user not being within HR, but involving a customer—that's a real and unanticipated benefit that they got by trying things out and being open to learning. Ultimately, this has become a cross-functional tool for business, operations, HR, and Finance to have an informed conversation with a customer on talent availability, as well as utilization.

In the business world Flex operates in, a competitive advantage is not so much based on cost, as on speed of innovation. There is something to be said for approaching HR the same way. The back and forth of iterative design feels a bit unique. It also means being willing to put something out there that is in development. However, this iterative approach creates a product the users really value in the shortest period. It's not always the intuitive approach, but it should probably be the default way of tackling an HR project in today's world.

Why "Test-and-Learn" Isn't a Normal Thing to Do

The "test-and-learn" approach sounds like common sense; it's about taking small steps and checking along the way to be sure what you are doing is working. If something isn't working, then you course correct.

However, "test and learn" can be difficult to implement for a variety of reasons:
- *Low tolerance for missteps.* When something goes wrong, is the company culture inclined to say, "This is great, we learned something," or "This is terrible, you messed up"? Unless the culture embraces the idea that it is okay if things go wrong, then it's hard to follow test and learn. (This tolerance for learning starts with the CEO.)
- *Desire for speed.* If you are pretty sure that you know what needs to be done, it's tempting just to roll it out rather than go through a more methodical test and learn process.
- *The unpleasantness of after-action reviews.* Even companies that embrace errors as a tool for learning find after-action reviews unpleasant. In his book *Creativity Inc.*, Ed Catmull discusses how people adapted to after-action reviews by finding safe comments, rather than insightful ones. He had to keep changing the format to keep it fresh.
- *The risk of saying "I don't know the answer."* In business, we like leaders who exude confidence. Saying that you want to test and learn can sound a lot like saying that you don't know what to do.
- *Lack of familiarity with this approach.* When Marketing says they need to run a pilot or Manufacturing wants to set up a test for new equipment CEOs, don't bat an eye—the idea of testing and learning is obvious in those contexts. However, since a disciplined test-and-learn methodology is less common in HR, it may be harder to get that investment.

Why Make a Commitment to Doing These Difficult Things?

I've just listed four reasons why it's difficult to follow a test-and-learn approach. Why bother? It comes down to the logic that if you want to transform HR, you need to make a move into the unknown, which means that you must mitigate risk. Since test-and-learn is the best way to mitigate risk, you must confront the factors that make it difficult. This is part of the method of embracing a CMO of People model.

What Can You Do Today?

After-action reviews are a concrete practice you can adopt that will help with building the foundation for a test-and-learn culture. There's no reason why you can't schedule a meeting right now with a few people who recently completed a project and have an informal after-action review on the project.

How to Run an After-Action Review
The core questions that drive an after-action review are:
- What was expected to happen?
- What actually occurred?
- What went well and why?
- What can be improved and how?

However, there are many useful variations of these questions; Senior Lieutenant Colonel Karuna Ramanathan and his team in the Singapore Armed Forces developed this 2–5–1 set of questions:
2
- Who you are.
- Summary of your experience.

5 (fingers)
- *Little finger.* What parts of the effort did not get enough attention
- *Ring finger.* What relationships were formed? What did you learn about relationship building?
- *Middle finger.* What did you dislike? What/who made you frustrated
- *Pointer finger.* What would you do better next time around? What do you want to tell those who were "in charge" about what they could do better?
- *Thumb (up).* What went well? What was good?

1
- The most important takeaway from the effort.

What Should a CEO Ask of HR?

Traditional HR might be just fine. (Thank you very much.)

Let's put aside the few bad HR departments that might actually get in the way of the organization achieving its goals. Fixing these departments matters, but I don't want to tackle this issue here.

In this book, I'm advocating for a type of HR function that is deeply involved in driving business success—that isn't the only model for HR and it's not the one most CEOs have in mind. What many CEOs want (and it is probably the only thing they have ever experienced) is a solid support department that takes care of details that they don't want to worry about.

In the support model, HR takes care of details such as ensuring compliance with laws around employee leave, handles the flow of incoming resumes, protects the CEO from headaches of managing legally required training, and so on.

HR's role in the support model is a bit like the role of a plumber you've hired to fix your drain. If the drain gets fixed, you're happy—you don't want advice on remodeling your bathroom. However, under the CMO of People approach, that is exactly the type of advice you will get. An elevated CHRO role is critical to decisions that affect every inch of the company—and if they think the bathroom needs remodeling, they'll say so.

If the CEO actively opposes a big role for HR, then you shouldn't fight it. The CEO must run the company as they see fit; if they need a support HR function, then that is what it should deliver. However, most CEOs have never seen the value HR can add when it is elevated to a higher role. They will be delighted when they find HR actively driving growth and share price; actively helping the organization overcome difficult problems; actively being part of the core team.

There is no question that people are a strategic asset (just like marketing brand), so when a CEO hears the phrase "CMO of People" it's easy for them to see HR's potential for playing an elevated role. I've learned from CHROs who play this elevated role that CEOs love when they demonstrate that they can add this kind of value. In fact, it goes all the way up and down the organization. When a business leader finds that HR can help them with a business issue, they'll eagerly accept the help.

Often this collaboration starts with shared data. For example, partnering with a technology leader focused on achieving the company's product roadmap milestones, we had to go back downstream to the predictability of the talent acquisition pipeline. As we reviewed the analysis, the leader mentioned that we have clearly "six sigma-ed" the process, understood all the market variables, and could now focus on the quality of candidates and the efficiency of particular channels to meet our objectives. This translates back into his planning ability to make and deliver commitments.

Don't make the mistake of assuming that a traditional role for HR is necessarily a mistake. However, you must also recognize that most CEOs might not have experienced an alternative and might not know what they're missing.

What Can You Do Today?

Think about the executive team, which would like to see a more aggressive and impactful HR organization. Who would prefer an administrative HR function that stays in the background? Can those in favor of an elevated function drive the organization in that direction?

How the CEO Contributes to the CMO of People's Success

What should a CEO do to get the most out of the HR function?

Assuming that the CEO wants a high-impact HR function, there are a few things they can do to make success more likely. Here are a few tips:
- *Get HR involved at the start of strategic initiatives.* Get the HR executive involved in M&A activities when you first consider the options. If the CEO thinks that HR doesn't need to be involved until after the deal is done, then they won't get the value they should from an advanced HR function.
- *Task HR with business goals.* The HR executive should be judged on how well they contribute to the business' success, not how well HR programs are run. For example, if the business urgently needs to cut costs (without degrading its capabilities), then the head of HR should be judged on cost reduction across the business, not how well they cut HR costs or how well they communicate about a wage freeze.
- *Get the HR executive involved with the board (and not just for compensation).* If the HR executive is only brought in on narrow HR matters—such as compensation—then it positions them as a specialist, not a member of the core leadership team. A nice fit for the top HR executive is, in partnership with the CEO, to define the multi-year organizational structure and related capacity and capability needs to ensure business results. Tying business results to strategic talent management is a great angle and is directly focused on business success.

What Can You Do Today?

Look at each of the tips—pick one area where HR's role should be upgraded.

Takeaways

- Many organizations have not been taking full advantage of the HR function; they should consider some form of elevated HR led by an unconventional HR leader.

- CEOs should consider bringing in someone from outside of HR to be an unconventional leader, while recognizing the associated risks.
- Leaders outside of HR should consider whether it might be a good career; if they have the right competencies, then it could lead them to an exciting job of helping to transform the company by transforming HR.
- CEOs say they want business-focused HR professionals but have not done much to ensure that the talent pipeline delivers the experiences that HR pros need to understand the business.
- Given the risks involved in transforming HR, it's useful to adopt a test-and-learn approach.

Chapter 9
How to Build an Unconventional HR Team

An unconventional HR leader might need an unconventional HR team.

Choosing an Unconventional Team

To get a broader skill set, source a different talent pool.

An HR department requires support from people with expertise in the traditional functional disciplines: labor law, recruiting, training and so on. HR cannot run without expertise any more than Marketing. However, if your goal is to elevate the HR function, then you will want an unconventional HR team—the best way to find that is to seek different skills.

The Three Top Skills to Look for in Unconventional HR Staff

The skills you look for in unconventional HR staff should in many ways mirror those you look for in an unconventional CHRO. Here are the three that are top of mind when I'm hiring:

- *Systems thinking.* Understanding how the different parts of the organization interact to generate results. For example, getting sales compensation right requires systems thinking as it is an incredibly important, expensive and high impact program that directly affects the company's bottom line. In order to be effective in that design role, you have to be clear on, among other things, the product and market strategy, the allowable financial framework, the goals for a particular reward period even before understanding the how and who to motivate. Managers, or critical team members, have to think about all of these factors at the same time, balancing for the best outcome, and not in isolation. This understanding means they naturally see beyond the confines of their own roles. They need to recognize that while they might have a deliverable for their job, it will have many different impacts across the HR function and across the company. To test for this, I'd often explain the CMO of People concept to a candidate and get them to relay it back to me. If they showed a sense of how things were interconnected, that would indicate that they had this capability.

DOI 10.1515/9781547400515-009

- *Collaboration.* A willingness to slow down and an eagerness to work with others. The systems thinker understands how different roles fit together, so they know they need to collaborate with others (even if it takes longer) to bring the CMO of People concept to life. To test for this, I'd usually ask candidates experiential questions such as, "Tell me about a project you did. How did you manage the project? What were you thinking about as you planned your approach?" Collaboration, or lack of it, shows up in the answers. In my case, collaboration was a skill I had to learn. My natural inclination is to go ahead and get things done, especially when I'm pretty sure I know the right things to do. Some good leaders taught me to slow down and involve others.

- *Curiosity.* A willingness to constantly learn, explore, test and iterate as a way of finding creative solutions. The word "creative" can mislead people because it immediately draws to mind the artist's vision. In this context, it's more like a curious engineer or scientist who wants to learn about the world and, in doing so, hopes to find fresh, creative solutions. It's only fair to note that the unconventional HR professional will often think around an issue only to land at the same solution that a traditional HR person would have given right away. However, without the curiosity to explore, they would never find those cases where there is a fresh approach. More subtly, and perhaps more importantly, the curious person is more likely to get the nuances right even if the core of their approach looks traditional. I didn't use special interview techniques to identify curious people; their curiosity tends to leap out in their conversations.

Three Other Skills I Value in an HR Team

Other characteristics I look for are:

- *Executive presence.* If you have a team doing unconventional things, then they need to have the communication and storytelling skills to sell those things to skeptics—that takes a degree of executive presence.

- *Data—and technology—savvy.* It almost goes without saying that an approach like the CMO of People, which is so rooted in data, demands that members of the HR team be "data savvy." Similarly, since technology is so embedded in every process, the HR team must be technology-savvy as well.

- *Risk-taking.* Doing unconventional things involves a certain amount of risk. You need people who can spot and seize opportunities, are comfortable with managing risks, and have the judgment and courage to shut down something that's not working.

Design Perspective

I've positioned design thinking as being customer-centric and integrative. Another element of design thinking is an inherent future orientation. When you imagine the team you need, then imagine it in terms of what you'll need a few years out, not what you need today. For example, if you are planning to go global in a few years, then you want to start bringing in people who are worldly and speak another language. Get the talent you need for the future.

What Can You Do Today?

Consider the HR team. Which of the six skill sets mentioned above is the weakest on your team? Look for those skills in the next hire.

Attributes of Unconventional HR Professionals and Where to Find Them

Look in unconventional places to find unconventional talent.

Here are some thoughts about each of the major HR roles, what an unconventional person might look like and where you might find them.

In all cases, the first place to look for HR talent is within HR; there are many HR professionals who have unconventional skill sets. If you can't find the unconventional talent you need within HR, then you should be willing to take a risk on someone with an unusual background.

Unconventional Recruiters

- *Some important attributes:*
    - o Look for people who think of themselves as a sales professional. Find someone who takes pride in knowing the company story, knowing their numbers and knowing how their numbers impact the company.
    - o They should be willing to ask provocative questions rather than just taking a job requisition and filling it. For example, they should probe to ensure that the requirements make sense for now and in the future; sometimes they should raise the question as to whether the role is even necessary.

- o   Seek out someone who understands that they are a brand ambassador for the company. Recruiters should immediately get that if the Glassdoor ratings from people who were not hired are positive, then that helps the brand and will make it easier to attract talent.
- *Unconventional places to find them:*
  - o   Consider people with a background in sales.

Unconventional Learning and Development Experts

- *Some important attributes:*
  - o   Look for business-oriented professionals who see their role as solving business problems, not as providing training programs. They will be far more effective if they think in terms of helping to deal with pressing business issues (such as missing product launch dates) rather than generic topics such as "how to manage interpersonal conflict."
  - o   Look for people who make a point of staying at the forefront of technology since this function is being turned upside down by new technologies.
- *Unconventional places to find them*:
  - o   One of the best tactics for finding good training professionals is to look for people who have held line roles in the business. They truly understand what the business needs and whether training will make a difference.
  - o   Consultants are often good in a training role—they have the strategic thinking, business-mindedness, and presentation skills to excel in learning and development.
  - o   A more off-the-wall choice is product marketers. They see training and development as a product and have the skill to iterate toward ever better products that meet real customer needs.

Unconventional Compensation and Benefits Pros

- *Some important attributes:*
  - o   For this role to have an outsized impact, the compensation and benefits pro must have the curiosity to look for new solutions and an innate sense of balancing what's rational for the company with what's compassionate for employees.

- They should see compensation as a means for driving performance, and should have a nuanced understanding of how compensation design can promote or inhibit the right behaviors.
- *Unconventional places to find them*:
  - Consultants often make strong compensation and benefits pros. Just make sure that you look for someone with four to seven years of experience in consulting. Someone with more years of experience than that might have entered into a revenue-generation role rather than doing real-world problem solving.
  - An alternative is to look for someone who has worked in benefits in a large company that self-insures. They are a good bet since they've confronted a lot more risk than the typical benefits professional.

Unconventional HR Business Partners

- *Some important attributes:*
  - Look for someone who naturally talks about things beyond HR and who can make the connection from strategy to the development of a work product.
- *Unconventional places to find them*:
  - Consultants are a good source of talent for people who will be unconventional HR business partners. Four to seven years of consulting experience is ideal.
  - Another good background is someone with an MBA who has worked in the operating business for three to five years.

Unconventional Strategic Real Estate People

- *Some important attributes:*
  - Fundamentally, you are looking for someone who has the vision to see how the working environment is a strategic advantage for the company in terms of recruiting, retention and (ultimately) productivity. Skills in collaboration, systems thinking, and storytelling are huge in this role, and quite different from the more transactional skills often sought out in facilities professionals.
- *Unconventional places to find them*:
  - There are venues called "executive briefing centers" that companies use to create an immersive product experience for major customers

in a controlled environment. Someone who has designed this sort of center would have the right kind of skills.
  o Alternatively, people who have done event management and have been involved in creating a particular customer experience will have the right mindset.

Unconventional Analytics Specialists

- *Some important attributes:*
  o First, don't confuse an analytics specialist with an HRIS professional, an HR reporting specialist, or a statistics expert. You are looking for a creative problem-solver who is good with numbers and can tell a story with them. A good role model for the skill set is the investment analyst who would prepare a report to evaluate a company's investment thesis. You're looking for someone who can create the model and synthesize a range of facts into an insight. You'd want a person who can collect a lot of data/insights, and string them together into an enterprise-wide story line with multiple sub-actions.
- *Unconventional places to find them*:
  o As long as the person has that mix of analytical thinking and storytelling, it doesn't matter what background they have. We hired a unique person out of a two-year banking program who had studied English in undergrad at an Ivy League school. He was highly analytical and a great communicator, which were the key skills even though you wouldn't normally look for English majors to do analytics.

Unconventional Employment Brand People

- *Some important attributes:*
  o A good employment brand person can synthesize a wide variety of views on what the company is about so that they can build an effective brand. For example, one of my staff members who took on this role did 60 one-hour interviews with people from across the company and pulled those disparate views together into a consistent brand message.
  o A related skill is the multivariate thinker who can see the parallels between launching a brand and launching a product, keeping in mind how it's positioned against competitors and delivers value.

o   Also, it's essential that brand people be highly skilled collaborators because they won't have the resources they need to do the work on their own. They need to influence the website people, the communications people and others to cooperate in activating the brand everywhere.

—   *Unconventional places to find them*:
o   There is a whole range of marketing jobs that could prepare someone for this job from the CMO of a small company, to the person doing product marketing, to a brand manager in consumer-packaged goods.
o   In terms of education, you'd be more likely to seek a Kellogg's MBA (marketing focus) than a University of Chicago type (finance focus).

What Can You Do Today?

See if there are any HR vacancies right now and then apply this thinking to filling that role.

Overcoming Barriers to Recruiting an Unconventional Team

Watch out for a number of problems.

The existing systems and expectations are geared toward hiring candidates with traditional backgrounds. If you want unconventional candidates, you'll need to overcome these two barriers:

1.   *Overcoming inertia.* The easiest thing for the recruiting function is to fill vacancies with traditional candidates. You'll have to insist that you want to see some candidates with unusual backgrounds and that the search should focus on competencies, not job titles. It can be helpful to come up with unusual job titles so that the inertia of routine hiring doesn't drag you into a world where you continually see the same old skill set. For example, if you advertise for a Senior Recruiter in Consumer Products, then you'll end up with a lot of candidates who have held similar jobs in similar industries. If you have a novel title like "Talent Scout & Evangelist," then you won't have to work against pre-set expectations.

2.   *Avoiding resistance from current staff.* It will be a disaster if your existing staff believes that their skills are being devalued. If the new hire's peers see them as an enemy, then you will be setting them up for failure. Frame the move toward unconventional hires as, "The existing team is strong, so we

can afford to bring in a new skill set to the team. You'll teach them and they'll teach you. All in all, we'll be much stronger with a broader and more diverse skill set across the team."

What Can You Do Today?

Sketch out a posting for a role that you would like to see filled differently in the future, focusing on the unusual skills and the type of background they are likely to have. Keep this advertisement handy so that when an opening does arise, you have something immediately on hand to push the hiring process off the usual track.

What an Unconventional Role Might Look Like

The CHREATE task force which I will discuss in detail in Chapter 10 "CHREATE," outlined several unconventional roles which they feel may become common in the future. Figure 9.1 re-imagines the role of an HR technology or analytics professional.

The main takeaway is that if we want to get more business impact from HR we should be open to reconceiving the roles.

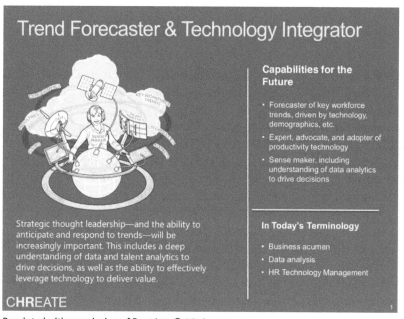

Reprinted with permission of Root Inc. © 2018

Figure 9.1: Figure 9.1 Re-imagining the role of an HR technical professional

---

Building Instead of Buying an Unconventional Team

Your existing team may have more potential than you expect.

The title of this chapter is "How to build an unconventional team," and since I've normally operated in high-growth environments, this has meant going out and hiring (i.e., "buying") new HR talent. However, this isn't meant to imply that HR leaders shouldn't or can't build an unconventional team from their existing talent.

HR professionals are well aware of all the different mechanisms for developing talent, and by all means these should be expected in building the right kind of team. However, there is one other aspect you shouldn't overlook: If your people all seem overly conventional this may simply reflect the expectations they've been living under. If you change the expectations, you will likely see changed behaviors.

What Can You Do Today?

Meet with team members one-on-one and ask how they'd design their part of HR from the ground up with no holds barred. See who has been hiding their unconventional views because they'd thought those views would not be welcome.

Takeaways

- An unconventional HR function will need an unconventional team
- Skills like systems thinking, collaboration, and curiosity become paramount
- Other important skills include: executive presences, data and technology savvy, and risk-taking
- You may find, and may even be more likely to find, people with unconventional skill sets outside of the traditional HR talent pipeline; look for people from different functions

Chapter 10
Contrasting Models for the Future of HR

Many people have written about the future of HR. How do these models compare?

Contrasting Models for the Future of HR

Many groups have proposed models for HR's future. How do they stack up?

The CMO of People model is not the only vision for how HR should operate—many people have proposed useful models. It's a good idea for leadership teams to have a sense of the different models being proposed for how to deploy the HR part of their organization. The CMO of People model is an exciting and proven approach to getting more business impact out of the HR organization. That doesn't mean it's right for all companies. Leaders should have a sense of the different models so that they understand the options and draw on the elements that are most important to their organization.

In this chapter, we'll look at these models:
- Blow Up HR (Harvard Business Review)
- HR from the Outside In (Dave Ulrich et al.)
- Beyond HR (John Boudreau and Pete Ramstad)
- CHREATE (a model proposed by a group of 100+ CHROs)
- Lead the Work (John Boudreau, Ravin Jesuthasan and David Creelman)

A Quick Review of the CMO of People Model

As a reminder, here are some salient points of the CMO of People approach to HR:
- HR takes Marketing as a useful role model (rather than aspiring to be more like Finance)
- HR focuses on business impact (not on the delivery of HR services)
- The head of HR is a member of the inner circle of the top team (not a second-tier C-suite role)
- There is an intense focus on a predictive, immersive, end-to-end employee experience that drives productivity (not a "be nice to employees" approach to engagement)

DOI 10.1515/9781547400515-011

- Analytics is a core tool (technology is essential to removing administrative tasks)
- The scope of HR is broad (it includes CSR, Real Estate and Communications)

We'll contrast each model for HR with the CMO of People model.

What Can You Do Today?

Try to articulate the model that your HR function is following today.

Blow Up HR

Does HR need to be improved or completely re-thought?

In July/August 2015, the cover of the *Harvard Business Review* flaunted the title, "It's time to blow up HR and build something new. Here's how." The most important part of the story was simply the mood captured in that title: many leaders feel, fairly or unfairly, that their HR department doesn't add value.

The frustration with HR is rooted in its lack of connection to the business. Some feel that HR mandates programs and policies that are at best a waste of time. In fact, it feels at times as though HR is actively getting in the way of the business that is trying to get things done.

Before we get too down on HR, remember that the Dilbert™ comics had a character called "Mordac, the preventer of information service," showing that IT could also have the reputation for actively getting in the way of the business getting things done. Furthermore, to some extent, HR's role must be a policing function that prevents managers from doing things that would hurt the firm (e.g., breaking labor laws, undermining the fairness of the compensation system). Still, the mood is behind "blowing up HR" has valid roots.

Peter Cappelli's View on Blowing Up HR

Inside the magazine, Wharton professor Peter Cappelli did not endorse blowing up HR—instead, he listed five things that HR should do differently.

1. *Set the agenda.* Rather than reacting to requests or complaints from leadership, HR managers should tell the CEO and operating executives what work-

place issues need to be addressed and how fixing those issues will improve the organization.

2. *Focus on issues that matter in the here and now.* HR should focus on company—and industry—specific challenges that the organization faces in the short term.

3. *Acquire business knowledge.* HR must learn to use analytics.

4. *Highlight financial benefits.* HR should use analytics to quantify the costs and benefits of its initiatives.

5. *Walk away from the time-wasters.* HR should stop investing in programs that lack clear impact.

Ram Charan's View

Management consultant Ram Charan has previously written in HBR that the solution to HR was to break it in two: one part that focuses on administrative duties, and the other that focuses on leadership and talent development. In the "Blow up HR" issue, he suggested that the CEO, CFO, and CHRO should form a triumvirate to guide the organization.

The reaction to Charan has been, "Yes, we get where you're coming from" followed by, "We're not convinced that you've laid out a practical path forward."

Comparison to the CMO of People Model

Cappelli's ideas are remarkably consistent with the CMO of People model and we'd endorse all of them. His five points are a good checklist for organizations to follow as they re-think what HR should do. In terms of Charan, I don't share his belief that HR must be split in two; while I agree that the CHRO must be tightly linked to the top team, the team should include other members of the C-suite (such as CMO or CRO) beyond the CEO and CFO.

What Can You Do Today?

Assess how your leadership would respond to the suggestion, "Let's blow up HR." How happy are they with the status quo? What's their appetite for trying something new?

HR from the Outside In

The best-known HR thought leader sets out a new model.

Dave Ulrich has been a leading influencer of HR organizations for more than a decade. His current model is described in the book *HR from the Outside In: Six Competencies for the Future of Human Resources*, which he co-authored with Jon Younger, Wayne Brockbank, and Mike Ulrich.

The most important idea in this model is the catchphrase "HR is not about HR" —great HR is about making the business better, not HR better. This is what the title *HR from the Outside In* means: you start from outside HR by understanding what the business must accomplish and then direct HR to those ends. It sounds obvious, but in practice, HR organizations are often obsessed with their own processes, concepts and lingo with little awareness of the ultimate "outside" reasons for HR's existence.

The following excerpt describes the six competencies needed to execute this "outside in" model.

- *Strategic Positioner.* This is much more than just "knowing" the business. HR Professionals must be able to position their organization to anticipate and match external implications and bolster their organization's competitive advantage.
- *Credible Activist.* HR Professionals must be internal activists, but they must focus their time and attention on issues that actually matter to the organization. They must be true professionals and be able to influence others and generate results in everything they do.
- *Capability Builder.* HR Professionals must be able to align strategy, culture, practices and behavior; must create a meaningful work environment; and must find and capitalize on all the organization's capabilities.
- *Change Champion.* Most corporate change efforts start with enthusiasm and end with cynicism. HR Professionals must help the organization counter that trend by helping it diagnose issues and learn from past failures.
- *HR Innovator and Integrator.* HR professionals must ensure the organization has the right talent and leadership for the current and future success of the organization. It must develop innovative HR practices that drive the talent agenda of the organization.
- *Technology Proponent.* All organizations seem to have difficulty in handling and transferring the massive amounts of information they accumulate. This is especially true in HR, and HR professionals must find ways to effectively use technology to understand and strengthen the talent within the organization.

In our view, *strategic positioner* is the most important of the competencies listed above; the central idea of HR is about making the business better. The second most important is *credible activist* because that's a significant change for HR. HR has typically been a service function responding to requests from the business.

The other competencies are more familiar to existing HR departments and will help them to focus their attention on the big things they need to get right regardless of their HR roles (e.g., training, recruiting).

There is nothing in this list that a CMO of People would say is misguided. The ideas of strategic positioner and credible activist are inherent in the CMO of People concept. Furthermore, it's encouraging to see that Ulrich's model emphasizes the importance of technology. What seems to be missing is the primacy of analytics and the value of the predictive, immersive, end-to-end experience as an overarching concept that continually pushes HR in the right direction.

You can learn more about the "HR from the Outside In" model by reading the book.

What Can You Do Today?

Get the Ulrich book—he's too important to overlook.

Beyond HR

A well-known professor and ex-finance professional, now in HR, re-envisions the profession.

Beyond HR: The New Science of Human Capital by John Boudreau and Peter Ramstad sees the past and future of HR as being analogous to the relationship between Accounting and Finance. In a simplified view, Accounting focuses on doing the transactions; Finance makes decisions on investments. Similarly, HR is currently at the transactions stage, and it will evolve toward a state where it makes decisions on investments in talent.

Beyond HR also argues that there are tools and analogies from other functions (including Marketing) that are useful for HR. For example, the book describes how the core marketing idea of customer segmentation should also be a core tool for HR.

An idea from *Beyond HR* that has gained widespread acceptance is the notion of a pivotal role. A pivotal role is one where an investment in the quality or quantity of talent will make a big difference in results. For example, if you are building an airplane from composite materials for the first time, an investment in the number and quality of composite material engineers will probably yield a high return. The composite material engineers might be no more skilled or important than the engineers building the engines; however, if the quality and quantity of the people building the engines are already high, then an additional investment in that talent pool is unlikely to lead to large returns.

Embedded in the idea of pivotal roles is a focus on performance variation. If there is a large difference in performance between the best talent and the worst talent, then an investment in shifting people toward the top of the distribution through better hiring or training will have a big impact. For example, if you find that your best cashiers are three times as productive as your worst cashiers, then an investment in that talent pool (e.g., more rigorous selection techniques) could have a big impact. On the other hand, if the best cashiers are only 15 percent more effective than the worst ones, then an investment in talent is less likely to pay off.

In the Beyond-HR model, HR helps the organization decide where to make investments in talent. It still has to do the traditional work of transactions, compliance, and so on, so the decision-making role sits atop the function much as Finance sits atop Accounting.

The Beyond-HR model is complementary to the CMO of People model. Combining these two models would direct thinking toward, "Where will an investment have the biggest impact on the employee experience?" and "What aspects of the employee experience have the biggest impact on productivity?"

You can read more about the model in *Beyond HR* by John Boudreau and Pete Ramstad.

What Can You Do Today?

Put together a small team of your smartest people (not just HR people) to identify the two or three most pivotal roles in your organization. Where would an investment in the quality or quantity of talent have the biggest impact on the business?

CHREATE

CHROs weigh in on the future they see for HR.

CHREATE (the Global Consortium to Reimagine HR, Employment Alternatives, Talent and the Enterprise) was a project run by a group of more than one hundred

CHROs and HR thought leaders who came together in a three-phrase project to scope out the future of HR.

CHREATE started from the premise that there are five forces of change buffeting the business world; their executive summary describes them as:

1. *Exponential pattern of technological change.* Technological breakthroughs will force organizations to adapt and reinvent themselves more quickly. Meanwhile, the workforce faces the risk of job loss and skill obsolescence, requiring that they adapt and reinvent themselves.

2. *Social and organizational reconfiguration.* The workforce's increased autonomy and decision-making authority will make the workplace more power-balanced and less authoritative. The workplace will be structured more through social networks and less through hierarchy. Work relationships will be more freelance, gig and project-based and less exclusively employment-based. Organizations will tap more diverse avenues for sourcing and engaging talent that extend beyond traditional employment.

3. *A truly connected world.* Information will be more abundant, richer and more available to everyone. Work will be accomplished from anywhere, creating a truly global talent ecosystem. Seamless global and real-time communication will lead to faster product development. Go-to-market strategies will be more diverse, and have shorter product and strategy durations. Organizational reputation will become a pivotal currency in customer and work markets.

4. *All-inclusive, more diverse talent market.* Multiple generations will increasingly participate as workers, today's minority segments will become majorities, older individuals will work longer, and work will be seamlessly distributed around the globe through 24/7 operations. Organizations that win will develop new employment contracts and hone new leadership styles and worker engagement approaches to address the varied cultural preferences in policies, practices, work design, rewards, and benefits.

5. *Human and machine collaboration.* Technological breakthroughs will produce exponential disruptions in markets and business. The rapid adoption of robots, autonomous vehicles, commoditized sensors, artificial intelligence, and global collaboration will renew the thinking about work.

To deal with this world, HR will have to reframe its focus and add capability. The change was encapsulated in four major roles for HR:

1. *Organizational Performance Engineer.* Diverse forms of "employment" and new ways of organizing and collaborating will challenge the traditional ways of working and require expertise in how organizations align, enable, inspire, and reward people to accomplish shared goals and deliver results.

2. *Culture Architect & Community Activist.* There will be a shift away from legacy, company-centric worldviews and toward increasingly considering the eco-system of all stakeholders—customers, suppliers, shareholders, "employees," and the community at large. This will require companies to more actively engage this broad community while prioritizing the importance of culture and brand.

3. *Global Talent Scout, Convener & Coach.* Given the changing workforce dynamics of an increasingly global, connected world, HR will find new ways to source, engage and connect talent in more agile, diverse, and effective ways.

4. *Trend Forecaster & Technology Integrator.* Strategic thought leadership—and the ability to anticipate and respond to trends—will be increasingly important. This will include a deep understanding of data and talent analytics to drive decisions, as well as the ability to effectively leverage technology to deliver value.

The commonality with the CMO of People model that leaps out is the importance of data and technology; it is one of CHREATE's four roles and matches the CMO of People's insistence that "analytics comes first" and technology is an essential enabler. Other than that, the two models of HR diverge in emphasis. It's not that advocates of the two models would come to blows over their differences; however, from the CMO of People's perspective, the CHREATE model seems to focus more on how we need to re-invent the specific functions within HR to face the changes buffeting the world, rather than on the broader principles that guide the HR function as a whole.

Where a CMO of People would find the CHREATE model helpful is in pointing the different parts of HR toward the future—for example, thinking in terms of a *virtual culture architect* reflects the fact that the organization culture has to work for people who are not in the office.

You can learn more about the CHREATE project at http://chreate.net/.

What Can You Do Today?

The CHREATE team was united in the notion that the world was changing rapidly and HR would need to change as well. Can you identify mechanisms that would allow your HR organization to learn and adapt? Do you need to give HR more room to experiment?

Lead the Work: Navigating a World Beyond Employment

If the gig economy is real, it will disrupt HR.

The Lead-the-Work model by John Boudreau, Ravin Jesuthasan and David Creelman is the most challenging of the visions for the future of HR. The most important idea in the book is that employees' jobs can be deconstructed into projects and tasks done by various types of free agents (e.g., freelancers, contractors, temps, consultants). This is often referred to as the gig economy, the on-demand workforce, or the Uber-ization of work.

The Lead-the-Work model argues that an important role of leaders and HR is to look at the work that needs to be done and turn up or down the dials on these three dimensions:
– Deconstruction: To what extent should work be divided into smaller pieces?
– Dispersion: To what extent does the work need to be done on-site?
– Detachment: To what extent does the relationship with the worker need to resemble an employment relationship? Can it be detached from that relationship so that the worker is an independent party?

For some work, the dials need to be turned down and it should be constructed as a full-time job, done in the office, by a permanent employee. In other cases, the dials can be turned up, and work can be deconstructed into small tasks, done anywhere in the world, by completely independent free agents. Each of the dials can be turned independently; doing that tuning, and managing the resulting arrangements becomes critical for leaders and HR.

The ability to have a "world beyond employment" is greatly dependent on talent platforms (such as Upwork) that allow organizations to easily find the free agents they need for projects and tasks. The new world is also enabled by changes in business models/mindsets and by a social shift such that being a free agent is seen as a desirable option. The success of this new model in any given country will depend in part on whether regulators enable or inhibit business from taking advantage of the opportunity.

The reason this model is so challenging is that it says that HR must focus on "getting work done" rather than "employees in jobs." Essentially, the whole history of HR has been about employees in jobs, so this is a difficult shift in perspective.

Digging a bit deeper, many of HR's skills are relevant to this new world—issues around finding, motivating and rewarding talent all exist in the gig economy. Furthermore, there will still be employees in jobs where the familiar world of HR won't change.

From the perspective of a CMO of People, this adds an important new dimension to their role. The tactic of a predictable, immersive employee experience that drives productivity will manifest itself very differently for free agents, especially if they are working remotely.

You can learn more about the Lead the Work model in the book *Lead the Work: Navigating a World Beyond Employment* by John Boudreau, Ravin Jesuthasan and David Creelman. There is also a good report on the gig economy in the UK by the RSA called *Good Gigs: A Fairer Future for the UK's Gig Economy*, available for free at www.thersa.org.

What Can You Do Today?

Try to hire a virtual free agent (using a talent platform such as Upwork) to do a small task you'd rather not do yourself (e.g., tidying up the look of a PowerPoint presentation). Does your organization make it easy or does it erect barriers to using the gig economy?

Synthesizing the Models

What do the models have in common?

The First Common Element: Elevating the Function

Most of the models envision an elevated role for the HR function. It is not just about being more effective or focusing on new things—it's increasing the centrality of HR in running the organization. Is this always a good idea?

One can imagine other functions—such as IT, Risk, and Marketing—making similar arguments that the future lies in elevating their function. Similarly, the most powerful functions—Finance, Sales and Operations—would argue that their centrality should be, at the very least, maintained. On its own, each argument would likely be persuasive, but not everyone can be in the inner circle.

It's unlikely to be productive to pursue the argument of "Who matters most?" since all functions are essential. Each organization must look at its own situation and, in particular, ask if a function is being seriously underutilized. I believe that, in many cases, that underutilized function is HR.

If your organization finds that its competitive advantage is in people, then the suggestion from these models to elevate HR makes sense.

The Second Common Element: Business Focus

I once heard an HR consultant relate the story of an HR manager saying, "I don't want to learn about the business—that's why I'm in HR." It's hard to imagine that being said in any other function (except perhaps IT).

Some HR departments are not business-focused because the function has its roots in generic administrative and compliance issues. If you are processing payroll, then you genuinely don't need to know a lot about the business, its strategy, its products, or its competitors. Secondly, many HR professionals and managers see HR as the "people people." A consultant for law firms said, "Don't you know what HR is? Those are the people you send employees to when they complain a co-worker has smelly feet." If HR's role, as set by the CEO's expectations, is to do things that don't require business savvy, then I shouldn't expect the function to have it.

It's fair to say the argument that HR must be more business-savvy is now old news. Today, many HR professionals are business-focused and get fed up by being told that this is something they need to learn. The counterpoint is that some are less business-savvy than they think they are; the experience of many managers is that HR hasn't shown good business sense.

The legitimate challenge for HR to being more business-focused is that the human dimension of organizations is particularly unruly, where the causal relationships between HR interventions and business outcomes can be difficult to discern. Expectations that HR can fix the human element of production as readily as an engineer can fix the mechanical elements are misguided.

The important issue is how the organization executes on the idea that HR should be business-focused. Execution depends primarily on who is brought into HR and the day-to-day expectations manifested by the top leadership team.

What Can You Do Today?

Go through the models and highlight the elements that would make the biggest difference to your organization.

Outside Perspective: Dan Schawbel

A futurist considers HR's future

When futurist Dan Schawbel, author of *Promote Yourself: The New Rules for Career Success* considers different models for the HR function, the first thing that comes to mind is the different environment that they will be working in (Note that CHREATE, discussed earlier in this chapter, started from a similar place by outlining the forces they felt were shaping the future environment).

Top Trends for the New Generation of Workers

For example, Schawbel points out that an important need for the younger segments of the workforce is flexibility. Flexibility is a more complex issue than it first appears. It is not just a matter of flexible work hours—it extends to flexibility about whether you work in the office or elsewhere, some flexibility about what employees work on, and even flexibility around the sort of workplace environment they work in. (That is, they've got someplace to work other than their cubicle—visit a WeWork office to get a sense of what the younger generation looks for in a workplace.)

The issue of working from home is particularly contentious with some companies reversing their flexible telework policies and requiring people to return to the office. Schawbel says this may be more an example of a failure to know how to manage teleworkers than a failure in the concept itself. It does take extra effort to connect at a human level, on a regular basis, with teleworkers, but if HR can enable that, then telework can be successful.

Another disruptive trend is a change in the nature of educational credentials. In the past HR could concentrate on credentials from colleges. Now all kinds of different organizations are providing credentials of varying quality. How should HR assess the meaning of a certification in math from the YouTube-based Khan Academy?

Perhaps much of the complexity can be captured in what Schawbel calls *the blended workforce*. The workforce is comprised of different generations, located in different work environments, with different employment relationships. This brings us a long way from a world where a one-size fits all approach to HR is effective.

Schawbel says the HR department of the future will need to be alert to, and ready to respond to, the many different changes taking place in the world, only a few of which are laid out here.

Bewilderment or Irrelevance?

A common reaction for senior leadership to these kinds of revelations about the future is that they're interesting and possibly important, but it is not clear what the impact on the bottom line would be or what actions the business should take in response to these changes. It's rare for a CEO to read about trends and take action—at best, they will pass the ball to HR and hope they don't need to think about it further.

What is the normal approach in HR? HR's traditional stance is to create programs and provide training. For example, there may be policy changes to allow more flexibility and training for managers to handle a dispersed workforce. Of course, there are a bewildering range of trends and possible responses, far more than HR can react to, and so they tackle a few that seem easy or happen to be top of mind.

The CEO may agree HR is doing things that seem reasonable, but they will not see it as sufficiently business-critical that they need to be involved. It is not sufficiently relevant to the business for anyone other than HR to care.

How a Business-Focused Framework Brings Relevance

HR should work from a business-focused framework so that it knows how to respond to the myriad of real or possible trends. In the CMO of People model, these trends will be seen in terms of their impact on how the employee experience that drives productivity is delivered.

If we think about the distributed workforce, then it begins as an analysis of a potential source of talent. In the past, we would have filtered out candidates who couldn't or wouldn't work in our location. If attracting talent who works at our location isn't a problem, we wouldn't waste time creating a flexible option. If it's important to attract new pools of talent, then one goes back to the talent funnel (recall the napkin diagram on the first page of the introduction) and thinks about how to change the funnel so that's it's pulling in, and not filtering out, remote workers. After considering the talent funnel, the focus turns to how a predictable, immersive employment experience that drives productivity could be delivered to remote workers.

You could expound on the options and mechanics for how to make these changes, but that would be a distraction. What matters is an HR function that can readily understand what's relevant to the business and can respond in a way that integrates with how everything else is doing. This has quite a different feel from simply adding a number of new programs that individually look good. Most important, the CEO will immediately be able to see the how what HR is doing will drive business results and, as a result, will have no doubts about the relevance of those activities.

Takeaways

- There is widespread interest in finding a way to reform HR; that's a sign that professionals feel there is an opportunity to get much more leverage out of the function.
- There are several different models to choose from or to mix together into a unique approach.
- Almost universally, people feel a core problem with HR is how it can become detached from the business.
- Changes in technology will likely have their own disruptive impact on HR, quite apart from any other attempts to reinvent the function.

Chapter 11
Conclusions

It's time to pull the threads together and prepare to act.

Summarizing the Pivotal Ideas

Create a coherent approach to the HR organization that CEOs understand.

The motivation for this book began with a belief that the companies I worked for needed to compete on the basis of talent. They needed people who were better than the competition, doing their best ever work, in a way that aligned with the needs of the business. Not all companies are like this—if yours is I hope the book has been valuable.

The second belief is that the way to deliver this talent-based business strategy is through a different type of HR organization. The HR organization has to be elevated: a driver of strategy, not a deliverer of services. Not all CEOs want this kind of HR organization; it can be a headache because HR doesn't sit back and take orders. An elevated CHRO asks uncomfortable questions that the C-suite perhaps would rather not answer. An elevated HR organization demands the CEO's attention. If your CEO is willing to take on this challenge, they can look forward to different talent outcomes.

The approach I developed to elevate the HR function is what I call the CMO of People model. I like this approach because CEOs get it right away—they know what a CMO delivers, and they can translate that to HR. Furthermore, there are a lot of Marketing ideas that translate easily into the HR realm, such as the sales funnel (talent funnel), customer experience (employee experience), and market analytics (people analytics). There are other models for elevating HR—this is just the one I know. While it might not be right for your organization, it is a fully implemented model that's been proven in business; it's not just a theory.

The talent-based competitive strategy can be summarized in the figure I presented in the introduction. The scope of what's packed into it should be clearer now that you've read this book.

DOI 10.1515/9781547400515-011

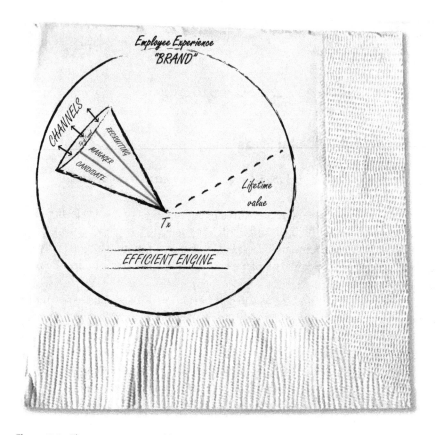

Figure 11.1: The concept on a napkin

The diagram starts with *channels and efficacy of channels* pulling talent into the funnel, followed by the various *stages of funnel management* down to the transaction (Tx), i.e., *the offer to hire.*

Once the employee is hired, it's about building the employee's lifetime value (eLTV) based on leadership, communications, competition, and social responsibility.

The whole diagram is underpinned—from the top of the funnel to the end of the employee's time with the company—by the *employee experience.* The concept of the employee experience provides a guiding set of principles that direct the design and operation of all the HR processes needed to deliver on this business strategy.

The value of putting this in one simple "back of the envelope" picture is that it shows that it's all integrated—it needs to be created, curated, and managed very deliberately where each step is measurable. It also introduces a well-defined vernacular from Marketing and Sales into a function that has traditionally been "hard to measure."

The CMO of People model believes that the organization has to create a predictable, immersive employee experience that drives performance. That slightly awkward phrase is not just a lot of nice words—each word matters.

–   Predictable means that the employee experience is consistent over time. Employees don't wonder what it will be like—they know and that removes a distraction.
–   Immersive means that the employee experience is consistent across all interactions, whether it is onboarding, a town hall meeting, the layout of the office, or the expense procedures. Everything (as much as humanly possible) delivers the same experience.
–   Finally, the experience drives performance. It is not about image or about employee satisfaction; it is aimed at delivering measurable results.

Too often companies think about the employee experience as a kind of window-dressing—something that looks nice, a bit of frosting on the cake. In the CMO of People model, the predictive, immersive employee experience is the cake. We take it seriously. We put in unending efforts to make it real.

When you start to unpack what it takes to make the employment brand real, the many implications just roll out. You need an unconventional CHRO; they need an unconventional team; HR must be unusually collaborative both within the department and with other departments; functions that impact the employee experience—such as CSR, Communications and Real Estate/Workplace Services—need to be folded into HR; people analytics must be a top priority; and a granular understanding of the employee experience from the very start to the very end must guide all HR processes. That's a painfully long sentence for making the point that the CMO of People has a lot of implications. The good news is that these implications can be spelled out and acted upon. There is clarity to the model.

It's evident that the model's major goal is to drive growth and profits. That's fair enough. However, if you are a CEO or CHRO, there's more to it than that. This model is fun and energizing; it's wonderful to see how it brings the best out in people. Personally, I could never go back to the old model of a service-oriented HR organization that simply does what the business asks.

What Can You Do Today?

Take a blank sheet of paper and sketch out the main ideas of the CMO of People model as they pertain to your situation. This is a good starting point before discussing the idea with others. If you need a primer to remind you of some of the model's more salient characteristics, flip back to the section "Contrasting Models for the Future of HR" in Chapter 10.

Four Ways to Move Things Forward

Here is how you might get started.

Find Some Allies

If you think the CMO of People approach has merit, a good step is to find allies who can help you think through its relevance to your organization. Most people benefit from having thinking partners, or even just people who are willing to sit and listen patiently as you practice articulating the ideas.

Allies are even more important when you get to the stage of wanting to implement changes—they can help you strategize an approach, identify barriers, and pitch the idea. As implementation begins, they will provide the muscle and support to keep the change on track.

Engage the CEO

Obviously, you don't embark on the CMO of People model without backing from the CEO. The one caveat is that you don't want to engage the CEO in the discussion until you've had a chance to think it through. Start with the allies, get clear about what needs to happen, get good at articulating your vision, and then go through the gradual process of getting the CEO to grapple with these ideas and ultimately throw their weight behind them.

Start Hiring the Skills You Need

Flip back to Chapter 4 on unconventional teams for a moment and think about the types of players who could most help you bring the CMO of People model to life. Even if the time isn't right to start making a big change, you can ensure that new hires fit the new model.

Get a Highlighter and Review the "What Can You Do Today?" Sections

I've tried to be action-oriented throughout the book; to sustain that discipline, I included a "What Can You Do Today?" paragraph in each sub-section. Re-reading these tips is a quick way to review the book and pick things to work on in the short term to begin paving the way for the CMO of People approach. Highlight the ones that are most relevant to your business.

What Can You Do Today?

Call up an ally to share a couple of the ideas that most landed with you.

How These Ideas Will Unfold in the Marketplace

CEO, HR leaders, and consultants who are inspired by the CMO of People approach will drive it forward.

There are three different forces that will help these ideas spread into the marketplace. The first is CEOs who know they are competing on talent and want to do things differently to get an edge. This is the easiest way forward—a CEO can run the HR organization any way they see fit.

The second force will be HR leaders and the professional bodies that support them. HR leaders will need to get buy-in from the CEO (as I've said more than once). However, from its inception, this model was built on what made sense from a CEO's perspective, so for once HR might find that getting buy-in is easier than expected. I hope that the community of HR leaders will share their experiences in implementing this model and share their refinements as they gain experience using the ideas discussed in the book. Feel free to connect with the authors on LinkedIn.

The third force for bringing these ideas to the world will be consultants. Consultants have a long history of playing a critical role in bringing innovative ideas into business. The CMO of People model has enough elements that companies will appreciate an expert hand to guide them. I hope that business consultants who understand the model in all its depth will work with companies to help them put it in place successfully.

It can take a surprisingly long time for ideas to gain common acceptance, and the traditional HR model has tremendous inertia. The one thing I hope is that people come back to the full scope of the ideas outlined in this book—without question, we'll see people touting "the employee experience" while seeing it as simply a way to re-brand engagement. So, let's demand that CEOs, the HR community and consultants build these ideas up rather than taking the easy route of watering them down into something inconsequential.

What Can You Do Today?

Is there a role you can play in bringing these ideas into the world?

Closing Advice

I hope you found some takeaways that will help.

Adopting a new approach for a major function is not for the faint of heart. It wasn't easy for Marketing to shift from a world of traditional media to digital media. It wasn't easy for Manufacturing to adopt lean methodologies. It wasn't easy for IT to move from mainframes to banks of servers and networks of PCs. If you are just looking to tweak HR, then the CMO of People model isn't the way to go.

However, if the model makes sense to you, you aren't happy with the way that traditional HR organizations work, or you feel the need to get much more leverage out of people, then you could adopt this proven model.

If you have a reasonable appetite for risk, adopting the CMO of People model will be a lot of fun for you and will bring a lot of value to your organization.

What Can You Do Today?

Share this book with someone, and then go for a coffee with them and talk through the ideas.

Appendix A

Chapter 2 introduced you to the concept of a "brand book" for HR. I mentioned there that we created a brand book for employees (at Shutterfly) and that it was one of the smartest things we did. The authors and publisher felt that it would be helpful for you to see an instance of a brand book for employees and that there would be no better way than to show you the current version of the brand book used at Shutterfly. There is nothing like a great example. In this appendix, we have reproduced the brand book used for employees at Shutterfly with their kind permission. The copyright remains with Shutterfly, but you should be looking at it for inclusiveness and organization, so that you can create your own brand book for all of your internal messaging and consistency of the brand, voice, mission, and expectations from hire to retirement.

The following 76 pages are the pages of the complete Shutterfly brand book. We hope that you will find them useful in compiling a similar document for use in your own organization.

Style Guide / 2013

DOI 10.1515/9781547400515-012

" *The achievements of an organization are the results of the combined effort of each individual.*"

—Vince Lombardi

Shutterfly, Inc.
brings our family
of brands together,
providing more opportunities
as we continue to grow—both
from a business perspective and
for you, from a career perspective.
As employees, you experience this
power of our brands every day and
are in the best position to be advocates
for our unique set of values. We want to
help you be the best brand ambassadors
out there, living and breathing our vision,
mission and core values.

This book should guide our internal
communications, including emails, online
collateral, internal posters and other
print pieces, in addition to All Hands
presentations, face-to-face meetings
and workspace interactions. It should
also inform certain segments of our
external communications, such as
PR, recruitment materials and
corporate affairs.

Most of all, it should make you
proud to be here and know
you are essential to making
Shutterfly, Inc. a great
place to work.

01 THE
SHUTTERFLY, INC.
BRAND

Chapter / One   *The Shutterfly, Inc. Brand*   *p. / 7*

* Shutterfly, Inc. is a family of brands in the
  business of helping people share life's joy
  We are proud to offer personalized photo
  products and services through Shutterfly,
  Tiny Prints, Treat and Wedding Paper Divas.
  Although our brands are distinct from one
  another, Shutterfly, Inc. shares a common
  mission, vision and values, encouraging us to
  have passion, inspire, act, commit and trust.

  Together, we are one family.

One Family*

The Shutterfly, Inc. Brand / *2013*

1.1 / The What, Why & How

We're a leading manufacturer and personalized products, offered

(This is what we do.)

digital retailer of high-quality
through a <u>family of lifestyle brands.</u>

1.1 /   The What, Why & How

Our vision is to
make the world
a better place by
helping people
share life's joy.

(This is why we exist.)

(This is how we do it.)

Our mission is to
deepen personal
connections with
the people who
matter most.

1.2 /   The "For/On" Principle

We work *for* SHUTTERFLY (INC) and work *on* the Shutterfly., tinyprints., treat. & WEDDING PAPER DIVAS' brands.

The "For/On" principle helps articulate the brand hierarchy for Inc. and our family of brands and sends a consistent message both internally and externally.

1.3 /   Family Dynamics

360°

Because our mission is to help people share life's joy, we want to offer solutions for everyone—no matter where our customers are in their life cycle. Wedding Paper Divas offers stylish wedding invitations and stationery, Shutterfly and Tiny Prints provide birth announcements and photo gifts, and Treat allows people to personalize their correspondence for all occasions through greeting cards. Together, all our brands share the same goal of celebrating life's milestones—both big and small.

SHUTTERFLY (INC)

A leading manufacturer
and digital retailer of
high-quality personalized
products, offered through
a family of lifestyle brands

Shutterfly.

Where your photos
come to life in photo
books, cards and gifts.

tinyprints.

Premium cards and
stationery for all of life's
occasions.

treat.

Personalized greeting
cards that really stand out

WEDDING PAPER
DIVAS

Wedding invitations and
stationery for every step
of the planning process

The Shutterfly, Inc. Brand / *2015*

1.4 /   Our Values

PASSIONINSPIREA

CTCOMMITTRUST

PASSION

Pursue excellence in everything we do

Please our customers to the point that they become enthusiastic promoters of Shutterfly, Inc.

Have a winning attitude

INSPIRE

Inspire customers to be creative and thoughtful with their memories

Empower ourselves and each other to achieve more than we thought possible

Motivate others by what we do and how we do it

ACT

Think outside the box and challenge the expected

Recognize and celebrate success

Lead courageously

COMMIT

Constructively challenge each other's ideas, commit as a team and then support one another

Say what we mean and mean what we say

Make the company a better place

TRUST

Treat others as we want to be treated

Have confidence in each other's capabilities and intentions

Care enough to give open, honest and direct feedback

Seek to understand, then seek to be understood

Provide timely communication to avoid surprises

THE
SHUTTERFLY, INC.
EXPRESSION

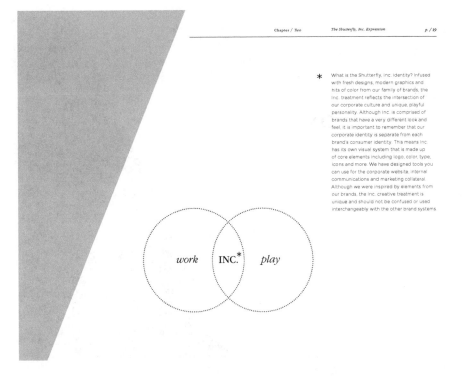

Chapter / *Two*   *The Shutterfly, Inc. Expression*   *p. / 19*

＊ What is the Shutterfly, Inc. identity? Infused with fresh designs, modern graphics and hits of color from our family of brands, the Inc. treatment reflects the intersection of our corporate culture and unique, playful personality. Although Inc. is comprised of brands that have a very different look and feel, it is important to remember that our corporate identity is separate from each brand's consumer identity. This means Inc. has its own visual system that is made up of core elements including logo, color, type, icons and more. We have designed tools you can use for the corporate website, internal communications and marketing collateral. Although we were inspired by elements from our brands, the Inc. creative treatment is unique and should not be confused or used interchangeably with the other brand systems.

work INC.＊ *play*

2.1

VOICE & TONE

Shutterfly, Inc. is more than just a company. It's a unified system with a common vision, mission and values. The best way to communicate this is through our voice and tone. This is how we express ourselves. This is what we sound like. Our voice and tone are a direct reflection of our personality and are defined not only by what we say but how we say it.

2.1 /   The Three Cs

Our voice and tone come from a place of confidence, as an industry leader in personal expression through our family of brands: Shutterfly, Tiny Prints, Treat and Wedding Paper Divas. We care about our employees, our customers and our community.

Shutterfly, Inc. is more than just a company—it's our unified vision to make the world a better place by helping people share life's joy.

And it starts here.

CONFIDENCE
CARE
COMMUNITY

Shutterfly, Inc. is more than just a company—it's our unified vision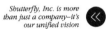

C[1] We are sure of who we are, where we've been and where we are going. Our voice is confident and professional but not stiff or overly corporate. We say what we mean, and we mean what we say. Our language is straightforward and easy to understand.

C[2] We care about our employees, our customers and our community. That comes through in our copy. Even though we are a corporate company, our tone is real and approachable. Our language makes our employees feel that they can trust us and that we're here for them.

C[3] We may be working on different brands, but we're all members of the Inc. family. "We," "team," and "together" are a part of our vernacular.

Shutterfly, Inc. vs. Inc.

❶ Introduce the brand as "Shutterfly, Inc." on first reference (and in all headlines and titles), and use "Inc." thereafter to avoid wordiness

❷ *Always refer to the brand as "Shutterfly, Inc." in external communications

2.2
THE LOGO

The Shutterfly, Inc. logo is simple and minimal. It conveys oneness with an unadorned circle. We are many brands, but we share a common mission and know we are part of something bigger. Our logo is the stamp of our company— a single graphic that unites us all. One company. One vision. One team.

We are Inc.

2.2 /   The Logo—Primary Version

SHUTTERFLY (INC)

The Shutterfly, Inc. logo locks a Gotham-based wordmark with the Inc. circle bug. The two work together to establish hierarchy as the parent to our four consumer-facing brands. The two elements, the wordmark and the Inc. bug, should never be repositioned or manipulated, though alternate versions are available for certain spacial constraints.

Wordmark   Bug

01
___
Clear space is determined by the width of the letters "INC"

02 /   SHUTTERFLY (INC)

03 /   SHUTTERFLY (INC)

04 /

DIGITAL   PRINT

120 px   1.25"

02

The black version should be used when printing or application methods prohibit using the primary orange.

03

If backgrounds are saturated or dark, the white version can help separate the logo from secondary surfaces.

04

Minimum size refers to the smallest size at which the Inc. logo may be reproduced and still maintain legibility. For digital applications, 120 pixels is the minimum width. For print, 1.25" inches is the minimum width.

Note: The Inc. logo should not be placed at an angle. (See vertical version for alternate formats.)

2.2 /   The Logo—Secondary (Vertical) Version

A vertical option is available to add a casual
feel when desired. Note: The logo is not
simply the primary version rotated. The Inc.
bug is rotated to allow the "INC" letters to
read correctly. This version should only be
used for vertical applications.

Logo Principles

When using the
vertical logo, make
sure it's always
pointing upward
with the Inc. bug
at the top.

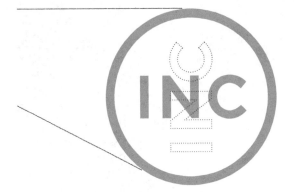

On the vertical version, the Inc. bug
is rotated 90 degrees for easier
legibility. This further enforces
the Inc. brand as the parent in our
family by emphasizing "INC".

Alternate Version

The condensed logo should only be used
when space constraints would render the
standard logo too small to be legible, like
in many social media applications.

2.3

COLOR PALETTE

Color defines us. Whether used playfully or sparingly, it's a powerful tool in communicating feeling and capturing the heart of our brand. The Shutterfly, Inc. color palette features a predominantly white scheme accented with Shutterfly orange and additional hues from our family of consumer brands. The consistent and repeated use of these elements helps differentiate Inc. across all of our materials.

2.3 /   Color Palette

The Shutterfly, Inc. color palette is centered
around orange PMS 1665—the same Ignite
orange used for the Shutterfly consumer brand.
It also uses colors from our entire brand family,
each including four other levels of opacity. As
a general rule, orange always takes the lead,
followed by white, black and gray tones to
establish an editorial feel. Pops of color from
the rest of the palette can be used to provide
additional energy to your layout.

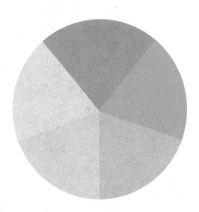

Pantone 1665 c

C: 0	R: 240	HTML
M: 77	G: 83	F05323
Y: 100	B: 35	
K: 0		

Black

C: 0   R: 0   HTML
M: 0   G: 0   000000
Y: 0   B: 0
K: 100

Pantone Black 7 c

C: 0   R: 88   HTML
M: 0   G: 89   58595B
Y: 0   B: 91
K: 80

Pantone 7449 c

C: 70   R: 64   HTML
M: 94   G: 24   40173D
Y: 43   B: 61
K: 50

White

C: 0   R: 255   HTML
M: 0   G: 255   FFFFFF
Y: 0   B: 223
K: 0

Pantone 284 c

C: 55   R: 108   HTML
M: 19   G: 173   6CADDF
Y: 0   B: 223
K: 0

Pantone 3252 c

C: 62   R: 85   HTML
M: 0   G: 195   55C389
Y: 33   B: 185
K: 0

2.3 /   Color Guidance

When choosing colors in the Shutterfly, Inc. palette, ratios are very important. White space is your friend and helps prevent layouts from looking too cluttered. Neutrals and orange provide accents, and the tertiary palette can be used to add pops of color when necessary.

The adjacent percentages are guides to help your layouts maintain balance and an even visual tone.

Primary
50% white

Secondary
25% neutral

Secondary
20% orange

Tertiary
5% consumer brand colors and associated tints

2.4

TYPOGRAPHY

Words tell our story, and the right typeface can help bring that story to life. Type can convey emotion, communicate messages and express the tone of our brand. Shutterfly, Inc. typography fuses an editorial approach with a modern aesthetic for a look that's both professional and fun. With a range of weights and treatments, our typefaces establish a clear hierarchy across all collateral—from content-heavy to clean and direct.

2.4 /   Typography

The primary typeface, ITC Garamond, uses five weights: Light, Light Italic, Book, Book Italic and Bold. The strong serif presence helps portray a more editorial look, and when combined with the secondary Gotham typeface, keeps layouts looking contemporary even when a large amount of content is necessary.

Note: When Gotham cannot be used, like in web applications, use Avenir.

ITC Garamond

Light
AaBbCcDdEeFfGgHhIiJjKkLlMmNnOoPp
QqRrSsTtUuVvWwXxYyZz1234567890&@?/#

Light Italic
AaBbCcDdEeFfGgHhIiJjKkLlMmNnOoPpQq
RrSsTtUuVvWwXxYyZz1234567890&@?/#

Book
AaBbCcDdEeFfGgHhIiJjKkLlMmNnOoPpQq
RrSsTtUuVvWwXxYyZz1234567890&@?/#

Book Italic
AaBbCcDdEeFfGgHhIiJjKkLlMmNnOoPpQq
RrSsTtUuVvWwXxYyZz1234567890&@?/#

Bold
AaBbCcDdEeFfGgHhIiJjKkLlMmNnOoPpQq
RrSsTtUuVvWwXxYyZz1234567890&@?/#

Gotham

Light
AaBbCcDdEeFfGgHhIiJjKkLlMmNnOoPpQq
RrSsTtUuVvWwXxYyZz1234567890&@?/#

Book
AaBbCcDdEeFfGgHhIiJjKkLlMmNnOoPpQq
RrSsTtUuVvWwXxYyZz1234567890&@?/#

Bold
AaBbCcDdEeFfGgHhIiJjKkLlMmNnOoPpQq
RrSsTtUuVvWwXxYyZz1234567890&@?/#

》 *Preferred style*

2.4 /   Typography Use

Note the adjacent use of scale, serif typography and added treatments such as all caps and underline. Always make sure that what you are saying is complemented by how you are saying it.

This is a _
headline.

"" Though italic cannot be used for headlines, it can be effective for quoting or emphasizing.

LARGER GOTHAM
FONT SIZES SHOULD STAY
LIGHTER IN WEIGHT

For general content-heavy areas, use Gotham since it reads clearly at small sizes. For general content-heavy areas, use Gotham since it reads clearly at small sizes. For general content-heavy areas, use Gotham since it reads clearly at small sizes. For general content-heavy areas, use Gotham since it reads clearly at small sizes. For general content-heavy areas, use Gotham since

By the way:

ALL CAPS & UNDERLINE CAN BE USED AS WELL.

BOLD styles
should also be
used sparingly
and never as
lead headlines to
avoid shouting.

Typography
Principles

1
Use Gotham for small type
sizes and heavy content.

2
Fonts can be ALL CAPS,
Sentence case, or even ALL
CAPS WITH UNDERLINE.

3
Paragraph justification
establishes alignment for
blocks of content.

2.5
PHOTOGRAPHY

Photography shows readers who we are, complementing our messaging and infusing communications with authenticity. Featuring real subjects—our employees and our environments—in elegant, understated black and white, our photography tells our story and helps distinguish Shutterfly, Inc. from our family of consumer brands.

2.5 /   Photography

Our Shutterfly, Inc. photography revolves around many subjects—employees, Shutterfly Foundation projects, facilities and events. By incorporating black-and-white photography and adding color with graphic elements, we can set a specific style independent of our consumer-facing brands, while maintaining consistency from layout to layout (since most of our photography is user-generated).

Photography choices can vary in gender and age of the subject as well as focal point, but they should always capture the spirit of our corporate culture.

Photography
Principles

❶
Use circles, squares or
rectangles to crop your
imagery for interesting
layouts.

❷
Color and icon overlays
add a layer of dimension
and energy to imagery

❸
Cropping into your photo
can make it more impactful.

2.6

GRAPHIC ELEMENTS

From arrows to angles, graphic treatments are an essential component of our toolkit. They support content, liven up layouts and add depth to our communications—as long as they are used with discipline and intent. Our graphics style is minimal and editorial. Copy and photography are always the focus, and graphics are used sparingly and purposefully to create a unified look.

2.6 /   Graphic Library

The Shutterfly, Inc. toolkit is grouped into
four main elements—arrows, color bars,
shapes and angles. These elements, though
flexible in implementation, should be used
with discretion and a sense of discipline.
Refer to the examples section for use cases
and design recommendations.

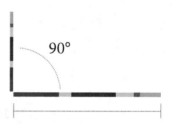

Color Bars

Color bars can work vertically or horizontally and can
accommodate different layout lengths and widths.

Note: Colors **in** the bar should never be adjusted or
changed in make-up.

Arrows

Arrows can show progress or direction and
call out important information.

Shapes

Circle shapes echo the Inc. identity and can be used
as an extra layer to highlight or pull copy away from
other elements.

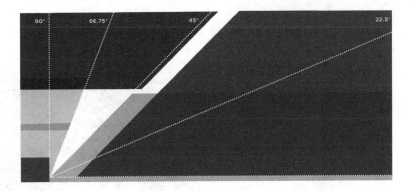

Angles

Angles and linework are based on five angles—0˚, 45˚, 66.75˚, 22.5˚ and 90˚. **The angles should always lean forward to imply progress and positive motion.** They can be mixed and matched according to the general look and feel of your layout.

(See diagonal line usage on the following page.)

2.6 /   The Slash

The slash element echoes the the "one to many" idea that is so central to our brand. Shutterfly, Inc. posesses many attributes—a work hard/play hard attitude, many voices with one vision, and practical products with innovative designs. The slash becomes a graphic element that has meaning even when used as a subtle accent in any design.

Slash Principles

Angles should always lean forward to imply progress and positive motion.

2.7

ICONOGRAPHY

Iconography can add warmth and clarity
to any message, no matter how complex.
Shutterfly, Inc. icons are simple, friendly
and expressive, allowing readers to navigate
our communications with speed and ease.
They can be used as helpful wayfinding
elements in user-interface applications or to
add context to copy-heavy collateral.

2.7 /   Icons

Our icon style is clear and direct and always uses the circle shape as its base. The content within is both straightforward and fun. No theme should be taken too seriously since clarity is the main priority.

The icons are primarily for marketing and user interface-based applications and can be used for wayfinding and to add visual interest in copy-intense layouts.

The icon library is created and maintained by Shutterfly, Inc.'s internal creative department. An updated reference library is available, as well as resources to help create new assets for your use.

Icon Usage

Icons can be rendered in orange, neutral or a pattern, as shown here.

2.8

INFOGRAPHICS

Infographics help readers process complex, data-heavy communications in a digestible and visually pleasing format. Echoing our brand expression, Shutterfly, Inc. infographics are simple and straightforward. They tell our story and communicate essential information to investors and coworkers, while always working off the basic principle that less is more.

2.8 / Infographics

The Shutterfly, Inc. infographic style is clean, simple and direct. Pops of color add accents while telling the main story, and though minimal in make-up, Inc. infographics evoke a contemporary style without being cold.

Above all else, infographics should be clear and relevant, avoiding superfluous use.

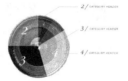

2 / CATEGORY HEADER

3 / CATEGORY HEADER

4 / CATEGORY HEADER

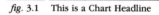

fig. 3.1   This is a Chart Headline

COLOR SPEC 1   COLOR SPEC 2

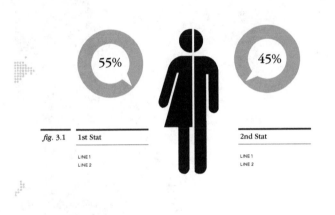

fig. 3.1

1st Stat

LINE 1
LINE 2

2nd Stat

LINE 1
LINE 2

Infographic Principles

1 Try to use circles as your main design elements when creating legends or complex shapes.

2 3-D objects can help tell your story and provide interesting visuals.

3 Thick and thin line weights help separate headlines from visual elements.

4 Iconography and symbols can add a casual yet professional feel to graph focal points.

5 Have fun with colors and layers, but do not overpower or clutter the information you are trying to communicate.

2.9

FOUNDATION

The Shutterfly Foundation is committed
to making the world a better place by sharing
life's joy in the communities where we live and
work. We strengthen the connection to our local
communities in Charlotte, Phoenix, Sunnyvale
and Redwood City through grant donations
and organizational assistance. Shutterfly
Foundation materials should capture this spirit
of connection, while clearly communicating the
details of our various programs.

2.9 /   The Logo—Primary Version

SHUTTERFLY
FOUNDATION

The Shutterfly Foundation loses the Inc. bug, locking up two words set in Gotham in a straightforward manner. The two work together to establish hierarchy, and they should never be repositioned or manipulated in size, scale or location.

01

Clear space is determined by the cap-height of the letter "S".

02 /

SHUTTERFLY
FOUNDATION

03 /

SHUTTERFLY
FOUNDATION

04 /

DIGITAL	PRINT
SHUTTERFLY FOUNDATION	SHUTTERFLY FOUNDATION
90 px	0.9"

02

The black version should be used when printing or application methods prohibit using the primary orange.

03

If backgrounds are saturated or dark, the white version can help separate the logo from secondary surfaces.

04

Minimum size refers to the smallest size at which the Shutterfly Foundation logo may be reproduced and still maintain legibility. For digital applications, 90 pixels is the minimum width. For print, 0.9" inches is the minimum width.

2.9 /   Foundation Elements

Though Shutterfly Foundation's core elements echo the Shutterfly, Inc. expression, there are some unique attributes defining its look, including the "do good things" heart bug, an element that can serve as a sign-off or main graphic for many applications.

PLAY ON.

....

....

01

The Foundation tone is casual and playful but doesn't sacrifice main messages.

Garamond and Gotham can play a more interchangeable role for high-level Foundation headlines, though the Inc. type principles should apply for the rest of the layout.

02

The Foundation color palette is identical to Inc.'s, but additional colors may be implemented depending on the message or event. For example, a Foundation event around the holidays could use our primary orange and a neutral, as well as a green or red tone to reflect seasonality.

Note: If a complementary color is used, it should be used to **complement** our core palette— not to replace it.

03

The Foundation graphic system is built around the Inc. slash, which can be incorporated even more creatively. Refer to the separate Foundation Style Guide or contact the creative team for more information.

04

The Foundation wordmark can be positioned horizontally, vertically or at an angle, as long as it is always pointing upwards.

THEMES
& APPLICATIONS

Chapter / *Three*   *Themes & Applications*   p. / 67

*   The following application examples reflect
how versatile our kit of parts can be, while
always maintaining consistency. Our style
guide includes many expressive elements
to convey the Shutterfly, Inc. brand, but
you should always make sure your main
message is clear and direct, and designs
aren't overly complicated for design's sake

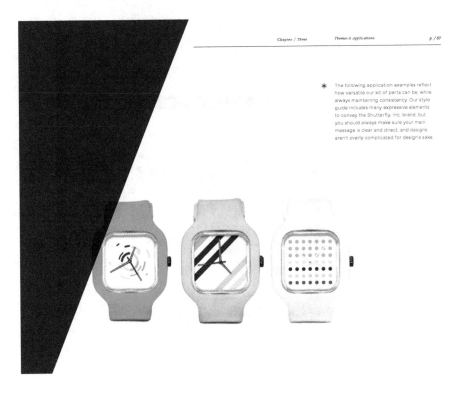

The Shutterfly, Inc. Brand / *2013*

3.1 /   Digital

Web Principles

1

Use clear typography
(Avenir for heavy content,
Garamond for larger
headlines) with white as the
dominant color for clear
navigation.

2

Interactive elements should
be utilized whenever they
can help clarify larger
amounts of content, such as
biographies or timelines.

3

When introducing color
to your layouts, orange
should always be the lead,
but colors from the other
brands can be added when
appropriate.

3.2 /   HR / General

Design
Principles

①

Use subtle hits of the color
bar when space is tight and
information clarity is top
priority

②

Make sure any underlined
text is clear and uncluttered

③

When using floods of color,
make sure to balance your
layout with white space

④

Regardless of graphic
treatments, the Shutterfly,
Inc. logo should always be at
the top of the
messaging hierarchy

⑤

As long as the Inc. values
and principles of design
are followed, there are
limitless possibilities of visual
expression

3.3 /   HR / Balance Concepts

$$\underline{\text{BAL} \quad \text{NCE}}$$
$$\text{A}$$

Thematic
Principles

Themes can help express
your idea simply and
straightforwardly. Strong
concepts let type lead the
way in your design.

3.4 /   Foundation

**Foundation
Principles**

1
Since Shutterfly Foundation
has a more informal vibe,
more liberal use of Gotham
can be implemented.

2
Partner with your Creative
team to develop new and
innovative approaches to
thematic events.

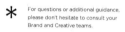

For questions or additional guidance,
please don't hesitate to consult your
Brand and Creative teams.

Index

DOI 10.1515/9781547400515-013

CPSIA information can be obtained
at www.ICGtesting.com
Printed in the USA
LVHW080039160821
695370LV00001B/29